Listen Hear!

25 Effective Listening Comprehension Strategies

Michael F. Opitz and Matthew D. Zbaracki

HEINEMANN
Portsmouth, NH

Heinemann
A division of Reed Elsevier Inc.
361 Hanover Street
Portsmouth, NH 03801–3912
www.heinemann.com

Offices and agents throughout the world

Library of Congress Cataloging-in-Publication Data
Opitz, Michael F.
    Listen hear! : 25 effective listening comprehension strategies / Michael F. Opitz and Matthew D. Zbaracki.
       p. cm.
    Includes bibliographical references.
    ISBN 0-325-00344-0 (alk. paper)
    1. Listening—Study and teaching (Elementary).   2. Language arts (Elementary). 3. Comprehension.   I. Zbaracki, Matthew D.   II. Title.

LB1065.O55 2004
372.6—dc22
2004010613

Editor: Lois Bridges
Production: Vicki Kasabian
Cover design: Night & Day Design
Interior design: Joni Doherty Design
Typesetter: Publishers' Design and Production Services, Inc.
Manufacturing: Steve Bernier

Printed in the United States of America on acid-free paper
08 07 06 05 VP 2 3 4 5

Contents

Acknowledgments

Completing this project was possible because several individuals put their talents together to make it happen. We wish to acknowledge these supportive individuals who worked on our behalf:

Lois Bridges, as our editor, for her insightful suggestions, encouragement, enthusiasm for the project, and for epitomizing what it means to be a real listener and writer.

Roger Eldridge, University of Northern Colorado Reading Department Chair, for granting us the time to complete this project.

Carol Combs, administrative assistant, for secretarial assistance and for keeping all of the children's literature selections in order.

All individuals at Heinemann: Vicki Kasabian for turning the original manuscript into this book; Eric Chalek for his superb copywriting found on the back cover; Joni Doherty for the interior design; Night and Day Design for the cover design; Kären Clausen for her assistance with rounding up a needed reference; Maura Sullivan, associate editorial director, for her belief in the need for this book; Leigh Peake, editorial director, for her support of the project; Pat Carls, director of marketing, and Doria Turner, promotions coordinator, for helping to disseminate this book.

And to the copy editor, Beth Tripp, whose work is truly amazing.

I'd like to thank Julie, who always listens to the ideas. Thanks to my Mother and Father, for being there, and listening all along. Janet Hickman (FMOA) who listened to all my ideas, good and bad, and was willing to laugh both with me and at me. Mary Jo Fresch, who is always there for support and to provide ideas. I'd also like to acknowledge all of my classmates and colleagues from The Ohio State University.

I would be remiss to not recognize my coauthor Michael for both including me in this project and listening to all of my ideas. I look forward to many more projects with him.

—Matthew D. Zbaracki

I would especially like to thank my wife, Sheryl, for suggesting the title that appears on this book and for helping me to understand the difference between hearing and listening. Specific appreciation to Doug Resh, research assistant, for locating and printing abstracts of research studies. Finally, I would like to acknowledge Matthew Zbaracki (RNM), for his willingness to coauthor this text and for his diligence.

—Michael F. Opitz

Introduction

The blank stare became a smile, which gave way to a laugh so deep her stomach convulsed. Tears soon followed as she gasped for air.

Such was my wife's reaction when I (Michael) answered her question, "So what's your next writing project?"

"Listening," I responded, taking a second breath to tell a little more about it. But her deep-belly laughter filled the room and overtook my explanation.

Dabbing at her eyes with a tissue, she was finally able to catch her breath long enough to say, "Good! Maybe you'll learn something!"

This book is proof enough that she was correct. In the process of investigating how we listen and how we can best teach listening, I came across many new discoveries. Imagine my relief, for instance, to discover that I am normal. That is, adults listen with just 25 percent efficiency (Hunsaker 1990). This means that as adults, we attend to and process what we hear just one quarter of the time! In fact, adults may be the worst listeners of all and, as Lundsteen notes, this is so because they have had little education on how to listen. This lack of education takes its toll, for as most know, bad habits can be difficult to change (Lundsteen 1979).

Other discoveries abound. The purpose of this book is to share them in an effort to help you better teach children how to listen. Did you know, for example, that children are often expected to listen for as much as 50 percent of their school day with little, if any, instruction in how to do so (Swanson 1997; Wolvin and Coakley 1996; Strother 1987)? In most classrooms, listening comprehension assumes far greater importance in learning than reading comprehension, yet we seldom address this essential ability, nor do we teach children how to develop and monitor their own listening comprehension. In fact, most of us rarely, if ever, consider the comprehension that is required of all successful listeners.

The truth is that listening comprehension begins at birth and serves us throughout our lives. We need to rethink our understanding of comprehension and extend and refine our definition to include listening comprehension. Clearly, expecting children to listen is quite different from teaching them how. The teaching suggestions offered in this book are meant to help you do just that.

To begin, you'll examine our definition of listening (not to be confused with hearing) as well as factors that influence listening. We offer some reasons to teach listening, the foundation of all the other language arts (Rubin 2000). We also explain why most educators ignore and neglect the teaching of listening. We then present some general guidelines that you can use to facilitate the teaching of listening. As you'll discover, listening has many dimensions. It is much more complex than you might imagine.

Chapters 2 through 6 each focus on a different type of listening and offer teaching strategies that you can use to support that listening. What links all of these chapters is the idea that for any teaching to be effective and have a lasting impact, it must be meaningful to the learner. This is one reason that most of the strategies incorporate children's literature and reading aloud in some way. What better way for children to see the connection among listening and the other language arts, especially reading? We also tend to agree with Moffett and Wagner (1992), who note that "activities that *entail* attention, as a preparation for action of one's own, teach listening skills far better than specific drills focusing on listening alone" (p. 74).

Make no mistake, however! Listening is the main focus in each of the activities because for far too long, it has remained unattended to by most. Demonstrating how to teach it brings it to the conscious level of awareness. As Winn (1988) noted several years ago, "The activities that enhance listening skills are readily available in the existing curriculum and are just waiting for identification to provide the opportunity to practice newly learned listening skills" (p. 145). No doubt about it! It is time for listening to take center stage and let the other language arts perform as backup.

We'd like to make another point regarding the types of listening each chapter targets: One of our key goals is to help children understand that there are many different occasions outside of school when we are expected to listen. One of the best ways to do this is to teach them to listen for a variety of purposes. In short, we want them to go beyond "school listening" (Funk and Funk 1989).

There are ways to assess listening, and these are discussed in Chapter 7. This chapter makes clear that to best understand how learners listen and what they might need help with, teachers should assess listening in authentic ways. The chapter also emphasizes student self-assessment because of the ownership it brings to the task at hand.

As a result of our research on this topic, we discovered that there are several sound reasons that we, as teachers, avoid teaching listening. Our hope is that by sharing what we have discovered, we can help all of us take a good look at these reasons in an effort to do a better job of helping children (and spouses) do what we want when we say, "Listen to me!"

Understanding Listening

Why define listening? What is listening? What are some guidelines that can be used to ensure the effective teaching of listening? This chapter focuses on answering these most important questions. These questions and answers provide the necessary grounding for reading the remaining chapters.

Why Define Listening?

Teaching something we cannot define is difficult because without a definition we are at a loss when it comes to explaining to ourselves and others *why* we are doing *what* we are doing. A sound rationale is purposeful because with it we are better able to choose specific teaching strategies and learning activities that best reflect it. It can serve as a guide when we seek out teaching resources and ideas to help us reach our goals. This is true with listening as well as with any other aspect of teaching. So why define listening? Because doing so helps us to know what we're about when it comes to teaching it to the best of our ability.

So What Is Listening?

Ask children this question and you're likely to get answers that range from those that focus on behaviors (e.g., not interrupting the speaker) to those that focus on comprehending what has been heard (e.g., learning from what you hear) (McDevitt 1990; Donahue 1997).

The National Communication Association (1996) offers this definition: "Listening is the active process of receiving, interpreting, and

> THE most basic of all human needs is the need to understand and be understood. The best way to understand people is to listen to them.
>
> RALPH NICHOLS

1

responding to messages" (pp. 1–2). The Literacy Dictionary (Harris and Hodges 1995) offers up two definitions:

> 1. The ability to attend to sound. 2. The act of understanding speech. (p. 140)

Without a doubt, definitions of listening are plentiful. In fact, Wolvin and Coakley (1996) discovered at least fifteen different definitions of listening as a result of their literature review. How can we make sense of all of these definitions so that we can move onto providing effective listening instruction? One way is to acknowledge that there is little consensus among the experts in the field regarding a definition of listening and to look for commonalities among the definitions. This is exactly what we did to write the following explanation and to formulate the diagram of listening shown in Figure 1–1. Commonalities such as these are drawn from several references, including Lundsteen (1979), Samuels (1984), Wolvin and Coakley (1996), Goss (1982), and Jalongo (1995).

A Workable Definition of Listening

Figure 1–1 is a picture of the definition of listening that provides the foundation for the listening activities this book suggests. It is meant to show the following:

1. *Listening is a complex process that is far different from hearing.* As Figure 1–1 shows, hearing is one of three functions that form a fuller view of listening. Hearing is merely being able to discriminate among the spoken sounds with little or no comprehension. As Doug Resh, a friend of mine, noted, "Hearing is a sound; listening is a thought." Consider, for example, the instances in which you were looking at an individual speaking to you yet were preoccupied with other thoughts. You appeared to listen to the individual, perhaps even faking it by nodding your head or making facial expressions. However, you comprehended little because you were focused on something other than comprehending the message.

Listening, on the other hand, is an active process that includes the attention of meaning to the spoken message. Lundsteen (1979) offers this workable definition: "The process by which spoken language is converted to meaning in the mind" (p. 1). Said another way, listening has not occurred unless comprehension has occurred. The listener is focused on answering the question "What does the speaker mean?" (Goss 1982, p. 307). The listener actively constructs meaning from both verbal and nonverbal signals sent by the speaker. Clearly, listening is an active process. To be sure, "A good listener listens with a questioning mind" (Strother 1987, p. 628).

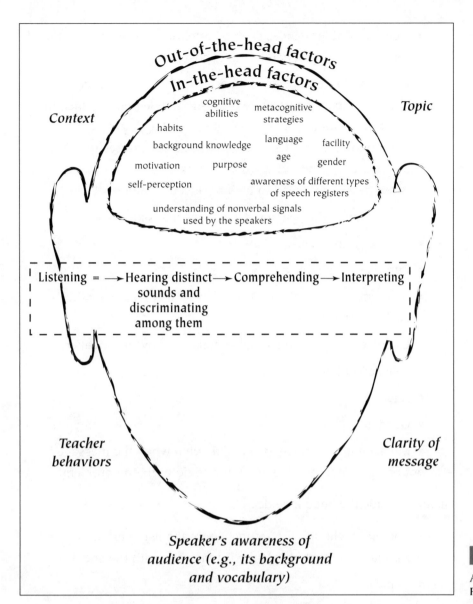

Out-of-the-head factors

In-the-head factors

Context

cognitive abilities metacognitive strategies

habits

background knowledge language facility

age

motivation purpose gender

self-perception awareness of different types of speech registers

understanding of nonverbal signals used by the speakers

Topic

Listening = ⟶ Hearing distinct ⟶ Comprehending ⟶ Interpreting
sounds and
discriminating
among them

Teacher behaviors

Clarity of message

Speaker's awareness of audience (e.g., its background and vocabulary)

1–1.

A Definition of Listening and Factors That Influence It

2. There are many factors both inside and outside of the head that influence listening. Factors inside the head that influence listening include

- Motivation for listening.

- Past habits. Good habits include listening for ideas rather than facts, judging content rather than mannerisms, concentrating, summarizing the speaker's ideas, keeping one's mind open, and questioning what has been said. Bad habits include paying more attention to the speaker's mannerisms than the message, allowing the mind to wander, permitting distractions that take away the listener's attention, overreacting to what is being said, and forming prejudgments before the speaker has finished speaking (Strother 1987).

- Neurological influences such as attention disorders, emotional disturbances, and prenatal drug exposure.

- Language facility, which includes the speed and accuracy with which the listener hears the words and the degree to which the listener understands the speaker's vocabulary, syntax, dialect, and anaphoric terms (i.e., words used as substitutes for a preceding word or group of words, such as *they* in "Sheryl, Julie, and Lois are here. They need to be introduced" [Samuels 1984]).

- Background knowledge for the speaker's topic.

- Cognitive abilities.

- Purpose for listening.

- Awareness of the different ways speech can be used (i.e., speech registers).

- Understanding of nonverbal signals used by the speaker.

- Self-perception.

- Age.

- Gender.

- Metacognitive strategies (i.e., knowing when the message is not being comprehended and what to do to fix the problem).

Factors outside the head include

- Context, including the setting where the listening occurs and the social relationship that the listener has with the speaker.

- Topic.

- Speaker's awareness of the audience (e.g., its needs, background, and vocabulary).

- Clarity of the message.

- Teacher behaviors, such as modeling good listening habits, setting appropriate expectations, and using effective classroom management (Faber and Mazlish 1987).

3. Listening happens in a pragmatic context. We listen throughout our day in a variety of contexts and these have an impact on how we interpret what we hear. Consider the many times throughout the day when we respond to the query "How are you doing?" If this question comes from a relative stranger or a mere acquaintance at work, we hear the message, comprehend it, and interpret it in the larger context. In this case, our interpretation leads us to respond, "Fine, thank you." We realize that the speaker is trying to be cordial at most. On the other hand, if we are having a conversation with a good friend who is concerned about our well-

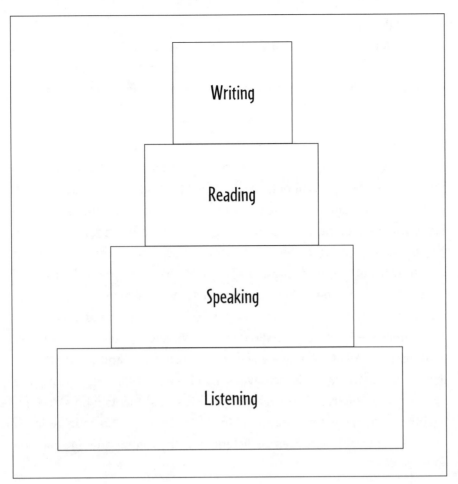

being, we respond in a different manner. True, we again go through the process of hearing, comprehending, and interpreting the message, only this time, because we are in a different setting with a different individual, we are more apt to respond with a comment such as "Let me tell you" and proceed to do just that. Clearly, "We hear with our ears, but we listen with our minds" (Garman and Garman 1992, p. 5).

Five Good Reasons for Teaching Listening

The definition of listening as shown in Figure 1–1 and previously explained provides the foundation for teaching listening. The learner's initial language learning comes through listening (Lundsteen 1979, 1990; Rubin 2000). Indeed, as Figure 1–2 shows, of the four language vocabularies we possess, listening is initially the largest. Given the importance of listening, then, here are some reasons for teaching it. You may well think of others to add to this list.

1. To develop an ear for language. One of the first aspects of listening has to do with being able to hear sounds and to discriminate among them. This is one way that children learn which sounds are important to their language. In short, children have to come to the understanding that there are specific sounds that, when combined, form words. These words form the basis for their spoken and written language. Therefore, when children are expected to listen to stories such as *Slop Goes the Soup* (Edwards and Coles 2001), they hear (and see) how language is used to convey a message.

2. To better understand and be prepared to listen for a variety of purposes both in and out of school. Not only do children listen a lot in school, but they also listen for about 45 percent of their time outside of school (Hunsaker 1990). And when you think about the types of listening we do as adults, you can better understand the value of teaching students to listen for a variety of purposes. For instance, when we listen to an advertisement, we listen not only to learn of the product but also to detect the bias that is being used to convince us we must have the product. When listening to poetry or music, we primarily listen to appreciate what is being read or played. Still other times we listen for specific information, such as what the weather is going to do. All of these types of listening have value and call for the listener to use listening in different ways. Lundsteen (1990) says it best: "The idea is to put joy from listening into the lives of students who starve for beauty just as they starve for food" (p. 217). Chapters 2 through 6 focus on these different purposes of listening with accompanying teaching strategies.

3. To help children better understand what listening is and isn't. Several years ago, I (Michael) discovered that children's perceptions of reading and the strategies they use when reading can have an impact on how they read (Opitz 1989). The same is true for listening. Some researchers (e.g., McDevitt 1990; Jalongo 1995; Donahue 1997; Tompkins 2002) have discovered that children often have a very limited view of listening. A first step in helping children expand their understanding is to become aware of what they are thinking. After all, change begins with awareness. Once identified, these views can be altered if necessary.

4. To increase learning. The results of several studies have one finding in common: children who are better listeners are also better learners (Lundsteen 1979; Elley 1989; Strother 1987; Pinnell and Jaggar 2003). In particular, children who comprehend well through listening do the same when reading. The reverse is also true (Daneman 1991; Lundsteen 1990). Likewise, because we can listen to up to 250 words per minute, two to three times the rate of talking (Foulke 1968), children need to be taught how to attend to the message and what to do with the lag time between the listening and the speaking. Without a doubt, teaching listening will help us maximize learning time. And let's remember this: "Listening is one of the primary methods by which children acquire the beliefs, norms, and knowledge bases of their society" (McDevitt 1990, p. 571). Clearly, listening is an important learning tool.

5. *To show how listening and reading are alike and different.* Listening and reading have many similarities. They are alike because listeners and readers need to construct their meaning of the text (either oral or written). Listeners and readers also use similar thought processes such as predicting and self-monitoring. Listening and reading also have some differences. For example, while readers can go back and reread if they failed to comprehend the message, listeners cannot. Sometimes listeners can replay a recorded message or stop a speaker and ask him or her to repeat something. More often than not, though, listeners get one chance to comprehend the message. Likewise, a speaker provides nonverbal cues that often help listeners better understand what is being said. Readers, however, are left to their own in this regard. Helping children see how the two processes are alike and different, then, can help them use one to support the other and call on specific strategies in order to best comprehend the message.

Reasons We Don't Consider Listening a Topic of Instruction

Given the five reasons we just stated for teaching listening, why is it that today, as in years past, listening isn't even considered a topic worthy of instruction on most occasions? In our reading, we discovered several reasons that were mentioned most often. Taking a look at the reasons and the fallacies behind them is a first step toward effective listening instruction.

1. *Listening develops naturally, so there is no reason to teach it.* Oh, how we wish this were true, yet we know it is not. If it were, why do we hear so many teachers and parents alike lament, "Children just don't listen very well"? Likewise, studies have shown that adults may be the worst listeners of all and that this is most likely the result of not being taught how to listen. And what of the corporations and businesses that devote such a large chunk of their time to teaching their employees how to listen to customers? Without a doubt, listening needs some explicit attention.

2. *There is a lack of understanding about what listening is and isn't.* True, there is some debate among those who write about what constitutes effective listening. However, most agree that listening is a meaning-seeking process in which the listener interprets what she hears to construct the message.

3. *Listening cannot be taught.* Oh, but it can! There are several studies that have shown that listening can, in fact, be taught and that other language

arts—reading, in particular—benefit from this teaching (Pearson and Fielding 1982; Boodt 1984; Buttery and Anderson 1980; Lundsteen 1979; see Pinnell and Jaggar [2003] for a review of additional studies). In fact, Lundsteen (1990) notes, "If a student cannot comprehend a message through listening, it is unlikely that she will comprehend that message through reading" (p. 219).

4. The curriculum is already crowded. While this may be true, listening is the mode by which children are expected to attain much of what they learn in school. Taking the necessary time to teach listening makes learning more likely in the limited amount of time we have with them. Further, several of the activities mentioned in this book demonstrate listening instruction can and should be integrated throughout the school day rather than taught as a stand-alone subject.

5. Practicing teachers were not taught how to teach listening. This appears to be the case for the majority. In fact, studies have shown texts used to prepare teachers to teach the language arts gives little attention to the teaching of listening. Fortunately, there are ways to address this issue. Professional reading is one way to keep abreast and continue learning. Second, the International Listening Association was formed in 1979 to disseminate information about listening in an effort to help teachers and others know more about the value of attending to listening. Visiting its website *www.listening.org* can be helpful.

6. If it were important, it would be addressed in the standards. With the emphasis on state and national standards, teachers often feel compelled to focus on them. How unfortunate for the children we teach, for there is more to learning than what can be stated in a prescribed set of standards. This is especially true as it relates to listening. In our own state, for example, listening is not regarded as a separate standard. It gets a very slight mention in the fourth standard, which states, "Students apply thinking skills to their reading, writing, speaking, listening, and viewing" (*Colorado Model Content Standards for Reading and Writing* 1995). Benchmarks fail to mention anything about listening until fourth grade, and even then the details are very sparse (e.g., "use listening skills to understand directions"). This is unfortunate indeed, for as we have seen, listening is perhaps the most important of the language arts.

For those who need standards to show proof of importance, however, the National Center on Education and the Economy, a nonprofit group founded in 1989, has issued a document titled *New Standards*, which clearly includes listening as a standard. In fact, the group has published an entire document that focuses on listening. Furthermore, there are at least twenty-nine states that include listening as part of their standards

(Goulden 1998). Finally, the International Reading Association and National Council of Teachers of English standards include listening in their overall goal statement. Their document also has terms that refer to the oral language arts in nine of the twelve standards (Goulden 1998).

7. *It's not a hot topic.* Rarely is there any mention of listening when one attends state and national conferences sponsored by the International Reading Association and the National Council of Teachers of English. Likewise, in our search for articles to use as references in writing this book, we discovered few if any articles appeared in *Language Arts*, a premier journal of the National Council of Teachers of English, let alone the *English Journal*. More were cited in journals published by the International Reading Association. Likewise, the silence that followed when I (Michael) told fellow colleagues what I was writing about was deafening. The silence and nonverbal behaviors, not to mention the change in conversation, led me to wonder if they thought I should spend my time writing on something of more importance—like reading, for example. One colleague confirmed my hunch by asking, "Why would you want to write about listening?" Regardless, given what we know about the value of teaching listening and the impact that listening has on all other learning, it seems unconscionable to dismiss it because it is not perceived as being a hot topic by the vast majority.

Suggested Guidelines for Teaching Listening

Children aren't the only individuals who need to experience success. We do too. This is especially true with the topic at hand. Generally, we feel ill prepared to teach listening or think we might be teaching listening just by expecting our students to do a lot of listening. However, as noted earlier, teaching children how to listen is quite different from expecting them to listen. Fortunately, there are some guidelines drawn from the research that can support us in our best attempts to teach listening. We drew the following guidelines from Funk and Funk (1989), Lundsteen (1979), Devine (1982), and Buttery and Anderson (1980); they permeate the activities described in Chapters 2 through 6.

1. *Set the purpose.* As discussed earlier, students need to understand why they are listening. They need to know up front what to listen for so that they can devote their energies toward achieving this purpose. For example, if the librarian is going to talk to students about how to get a library card, the teacher can tell the students ahead of time that the librarian is coming for a visit and that he will be stating three steps necessary to obtain a library card. The teacher can then instruct the students to listen for the three specific steps. A variation of this would be to have students

state what they think the three steps might be and listen to learn if what they predicted matches what the librarian has to say. The main point, then, is that children need to be guided, which will increase their learning from listening. Once the presentation is finished, the teacher can ask her students to write or tell what they discovered and use their responses as a comprehension check.

2. *Set the stage.* Children need to get ready to listen. Perhaps the first step toward getting them ready is to set expectations. They need to know that you expect them to listen in a specific way. Once you have set expectations, you need to create the appropriate atmosphere. Stopping an earlier activity, eliminating background noise and other distractions, arranging seats appropriately, stating a purpose for listening, and telling students what will happen after the listening experience are all ways to set the stage for active listening.

3. *Provide follow-up.* Once the listening experience has occurred, students need to be held accountable for whatever it was that they were to attend to. To ensure student success, the follow-up needs to happen right after the listening experience. These follow-up activities permit children to show what they learned. They can also serve as authentic assessments. Which children were able to achieve the stated purpose? Which children need additional help? Are there any children who have misconceptions of what the speaker stated?

One word of caution is in order here. There are several follow-up activities that can be used for any given listening experience. Choosing an appropriate one is crucial. Choose one that best fits the listening experience. In our university courses, for example, we often have students fill in a listening guide we provide before watching a video. We also let them know before we show the video that they will be expected to show understanding by sharing one essential point with others after watching the video. Sometimes we have them do this orally, whereas other times they provide a written response. In either case, the activity fits well with the listening experience. *Meaningful* is the key word here.

4. *Keep it brief.* As discussed earlier, students are expected to listen for a good part of the school day with little instruction in how to do so. There are also students for whom listening is very difficult because it is not their favored learning modality. With these students in mind, teachers should keep listening experiences focused and relatively short. This will help guard against children tuning out because they are expected to listen too long.

5. *Integrate it!* For children to fully understand how to listen, they need to see that listening is used to accomplish a specific purpose in a variety

of subject areas. In other words, the listening experience needs to be as authentic as possible because the more meaningful it is to the learner, the more likely it is that the learner will be able to make sense of it. Listening experiences can occur with the whole class or in small-group settings. Regardless, keeping the experience integrated with ongoing activities is crucial.

6. Be a model. If we want children to become better listeners, we need to be better listeners ourselves. (You might want to visit the International Listening Association's website, *www.listening.org*, to take the listening profile shown there. It will give you an idea about how well you currently listen.) If we want children to show a speaker respect through careful listening, we need to do the same. Lundsteen (1990) offers us this pertinent thought: "Listening is not only the heart of human interaction, but also the heart of teaching and learning" (p. 213).

7. Avoid repeating yourself and/or student responses. One of the ways that listening can be reinforced is to say something once and only once. Initially, this can be difficult on everyone if you have been repeating what you say. However, in the long run, students will listen with greater ease. Children can and should be expected to restate questions and answer questions posed by one another, for this is one way to show them that they need to listen to one another as well as the teacher.

Figure 1–3 provides an overview of the types of listening, the teaching strategies that coincide with each type, and the skills that each strategy develops. Chapters 2 through 6 each showcase a different type of listening and offer explanations of the various strategies.

SKILLS/STRATEGIES	DISCRIMINATIVE					PRECISE					STRATEGIC					CRITICAL					APPRECIATIVE				
	Tongue-Tying Twisters	How Do I Feel?	Loud or Soft Sounds?	"Hey Now, What's That Sound?"	Show Me	Give Me Five	What's the Good Word?	Talk Show	Add One	Are You Following?	Fill in the Gaps	DLTA	SLA	Sum It Up!	Get the Picture	What's Your Perspective?	Loaded Words	Propaganda	Fact and Opinion	Compare and Contrast	Humor	Poetry	Music	Multimedia	Theatre
phonological awareness	•			•																					
vocal expression		•	•	•																					
onomatopoeia	•		•	•																					
nonverbal clues			•		•																				
associating words and meanings							•																		
deducing the meaning of words from context							•																		
understanding grammatical structures							•			•															
forming sensory impressions								•	•																
recalling details						•		•	•																
recalling sequences						•		•	•																
paraphrasing information						•		•	•																
following directions										•															
recognizing multiple characters								•	•	•															
connecting ideas and information											•	•		•											
connecting prior knowledge with new info															•										
summarizing											•	•		•											
predicting												•		•											
asking questions													•												
inferencing											•														
distinguishing between inferences and factual information														•											

identifying implied main ideas

classifying and organizing information

recognizing emotive language

recognizing bias

distinguishing between fact and opinion

recognizing speaker's inferences

evaluating sources

detecting propaganda devices

determining relevant information

recognizes physical attributes evoked

recognizes what he/she appreciates and why

gains experience listening in a variety of forms

recognizes the pleasure listening can bring

aware of the different elements while listening

recognizes feelings or mood that is evoked

recognizes the power of language

appreciates the conciseness of language

appreciates how words flow from speaker

appreciates oral interpretations

appreciates how music and other performing arts work together to evoke feeling

understands the power of imagination

1–3.

Effective Listening Strategies and the Skills They Develop

2

Discriminative Listening

Sounds surround us. Knowing which to attend to and those to ignore is what enables us to function in our environment. Consider, for example, infants who discriminate among the various speech sounds to develop an ear for their language. And how about the children who can tune out background noises such as music when they are engaged in another task that requires their full attention? They, too, are discriminating among sounds. Clearly, children, like adults, learn to discriminate among different sounds in order to function in their environments.

But discriminative listening is more than distinguishing among sounds in a language or an environment; it also involves paying attention to nonverbal cues provided by speakers (Wolvin and Coakley 1996, 1979). We can tell, for instance, how an individual might be feeling based on facial expressions as well as other forms of body language. A clenched fist, for example, might indicate anger. As it relates to school, a nonverbal cue such as writing something on the board for students to see most often indicates that the information is important.

Learning to distinguish verbal and nonverbal cues is a matter of discriminative listening. It is the first type of listening we address because it is the foundation of the other purposes for listening featured in succeeding chapters. To paraphrase Wolvin and Coakley (1996), individuals who are adept at discriminative listening and are listening for specific ideas and details (i.e., precise listening, explained in Chapter 3) are in a better position to note when a change in voice happens. They can therefore make some decisions about the speaker's message. As a result of listening to how the speaker uses vocal expressions or nonverbal cues

SKILL	TONGUE-TYING TWISTERS	HOW DO I FEEL?	LOUD OR SOFT SOUNDS?	HEY NOW, WHAT'S THAT SOUND?	SHOW ME
Phonological awareness	•			•	
Vocal expression		•	•	•	
Onomatopoeia	•		•	•	
Nonverbal cues			•		•

2–1.

Effective Discriminative-Listening Teaching Strategies and the Skills They Develop

such as hand gestures, strategic listeners (see Chapter 4) use discriminative listening to make inferences or to visualize. Critical listeners (see Chapter 5) use discriminative-listening attributes such as facial expressions and body movements to better determine the speaker's perspective on a given topic. Finally, being able to distinguish among sounds can help appreciative listeners (see Chapter 6) enjoy a recited poem, a favorite singer, or a favorite song.

This chapter provides teaching suggestions to help students be better discriminating listeners. Tongue-Tying Twisters (pp. 16–18) shows children the redundancy of sounds in their language and how they can use repeating sounds in fun ways. How Do I Feel? (pp. 19–21) provides children with an opportunity to learn how to use their voices to convey their feelings. Loud or Soft Sounds (pp. 22–24) is a way to help children become more sensitive to the sounds in their environment. Hey Now, What's That Sound? (pp. 25–27) helps children listen for words that describe sounds associated with them (i.e., onomatopoeia). And after experiencing Show Me (pp. 28–30), children will better understand how listeners need to pay attention to the speaker's nonverbal cues. Figure 2–1 lists these suggestions and the specific listening skills each develops.

TONGUE-TYING TWISTERS

GRADE LEVEL: K-2

Description

Perhaps one of the best ways for children to develop phonological awareness is through discriminative listening. The listener must discriminate among sounds in order to focus on specific identified sounds. There are many tasks associated with phonological awareness in general and phonemic awareness in particular (see Opitz [2000] for a detailed explanation of these many tasks). This particular activity asks students to use discriminative listening to notice that all words within a sentence begin with the same sound (i.e., alliteration). Once they have listened to the story and reviewed alliteration, students create their own alliterative sentences.

Teaching Suggestions

1. Choose a children's literature selection that focuses on alliteration.

2. Read the book aloud to children.

3. Tell children that you will now reread something from the book and they need to listen for how each word in the sentence is alike.

4. Reread the sentence from the text.

5. Invite children to tell what they heard.

6. Invite children to make up a class tongue twister based on the sound you provide.

7. Have children create their own tongue twisters.

Suggested Titles and Language Features They Use

Giles Andreae, *K Is for Kissing a Cool Kangaroo* (rhyme)

Marion Dane Bauer, *Why Do Kittens Purr?* (repetition)

Sandra Gilbert Brug, *Soccer Beat* (rhyme)

Joy Cowley, *Mrs. Wishy-Washy's Farm* (repetition)

Dayle Ann Dodds, *Where's Pup?*

Valorie Fisher, *Ellsworth's Extraordinary Electric Ears* (alliteration)

Rachel Isadora, *Not Just Tutus* (rhyme)

Stephen Michael King, *Emily Loves to Bounce* (rhyme)

Bob Kolar, *Racer Dogs*

Bill Martin Jr., *Panda Bear, Panda Bear, What Do You See?* (rhyme and repetition)

Tony Mitton, *Dinosaurumpus!*

Patricia Poloacco, *G Is for Goat* (rhyme)

Deborah Lee Rose, *One Nighttime Sea* (rhyme)

Teacher Voice

To help advance students' understanding of phoneme matching, Sheryl decides to use *Ellsworth's Extraordinary Electric Ears*. The author uses alliteration to write an anecdote for each letter of the alphabet. Sheryl first reads the book to the class for sheer enjoyment. Once she has read the book, she returns to the second page and asks children to listen carefully as she rereads it. Because she knows that she needs to set a purpose for listening, she tells students that they need to listen to how each word in the sentence begins. After reading the sentence, she asks students to tell her how each word started (i.e., phoneme matching). After students have shared their ideas, Sheryl suggests that they create a tongue twister together. She gives the /m/ sound and children join together to create the following tongue twister: Matthew made meatballs. Sheryl then has students create their own tongue twisters to share with others. As they are leaving the whole-group area, Sheryl reminds students that sounds are an important part of their language. Paying attention to them can be a way to learn important sounds and how to play with sounds.

Extensions/Tips/Connections

1. An additional way to help children match sounds is to invite them to bring in objects from home that begin with a given sound. Display all objects on a table in the classroom. Next, have children use some of the objects to create an alliterative sentence.

2. Yet another way to help children learn to match sounds is to have them make a sound collage. Using magazines, invite children to find pictures of objects that have the same beginning sound. Children can cut and paste the pictures onto a piece of construction paper.

3. Another phonological awareness task is phoneme substitution. Using a book such as *K Is for Kissing a Cool Kangaroo*, state two words that rhyme and ask children to tell you what needs to be changed in the first word to create the rhyming second word. For example, you might say something like this: "What sounds do we need to change to make *dream* into *cream*?" (Take away the /d/ and substitute /c/.)

How DO I FEEL?

GRADE LEVEL: K-6

Description

How speakers use their voices when speaking is one factor that influences listening (Samuels 1984). A speaker who uses much expression and animation indirectly encourages the audience to listen, to stay engaged, and to comprehend the intended message. Listeners can also gain a better understanding of the characters in a story when they know how to discriminate among the ways the readers use their voices. How Do I Feel? is designed to provide children with some practice in using discriminative listening to better understand the speaker's message.

Teaching Suggestions

1. Choose a children's literature selection to read aloud.

2. Read the book aloud to the students two times. The first time, read it in monotone voice. In the second reading, read with expression as cued by the author's use of print and punctuation.

3. Ask students what they noticed about your readings of the story. If needed, point out that the size of print and the punctuation helped you know how to read the story.

4. Invite students to state which reading caused them to want to listen to the story.

5. Remind children that what readers say and how readers say it help the listeners better understand the story characters and how they might be feeling.

6. Provide children with time to practice this skill by having them prepare a section or a few sentences from a book to share with an interested audience.

Suggested Titles

Linda Ashman, *Rub-a-Dub-Dub*

Robert Florczak, *Yikes!!!*

Marla Frazee, *Roller Coaster*

Tony Johnston, *Go Track a Yak*

Rukhsana Khan, *Ruler of the Courtyard*

Jarrett Krosoczka, *Bubble Bath Pirates!*

Roni Schotter, *Captain Bob Takes Flight*

Pat Thompson, *Drat That Fat Cat*

Lisa Wheeler, *One Dark Night*

Karma Wilson, *Bear Wants More*

Teacher Voice

Several observations led Julie to the conclusion that several of her second graders needed to learn how to engage listeners by reading with expression. She decided that she would use *Yikes!!!* for a demonstration because its print sizes and use of punctuation signal the reader to do something with her voice. After explaining to students that the purpose for the listening was to see which way interested them most, Julie read the story two times. The first time through, she read in a monotone voice. During the second reading, she attended to the typographical cues. Consequently, she used much expression. After reading, she asked students which reading they liked best and which caused them to keep listening. Student responses were unanimous: they liked the second way much better. They felt like they could better understand the character, too. Julie closed the listening lesson by telling students that as listeners, they could gain much by focusing on how the speaker uses his voice. She also pointed out that speakers could have an impact on how well the audience listens.

Extensions/Tips/Connections

1. *Bubble Bath Pirates!* is an excellent book to use context to help listeners determine which voice or voices to use for given characters. Because the book is about pirates, all readers need to convey this to listeners through the use of pirate voices. Through pirate voices, listeners will unearth the hidden treasures of discriminative listening.

2. After becoming familiar with several story characters, Matthew blindfolded a student volunteer and selected another student in the classroom to be a story character. The student selected to be a

story character then spoke like the character from the familiar book. The blindfolded student had to guess which character the other student was portraying. With the blindfold, the student had to rely solely on discriminative listening to determine the correct story character.

3. Although discriminative listening is one of the most basic types of listening, this need not mean that it ends with kindergarten. One way of extending this teaching idea into the upper grades is to use books that appeal to the specific grade level you are working with. The sophistication of the text changes but the basic teaching strategy remains the same, as does the importance of using expression as a means of engaging the listener.

LOUD OR SOFT SOUNDS?

GRADE LEVEL: K-6

Description

The crash of thunder and the sound of snow falling on the ground are two different sounds; one is loud, the other soft. Young children may have recognized them in isolation but not compared the two. Loud or Soft Sounds? helps students identify the different sounds they know and use discriminative listening to tell which are loud and which are soft. While the main focus is on discriminative listening, students can also think more critically (see Chapter 5) as they listen to determine how some sounds fit more easily in specific categories.

Teaching Suggestions

1. Choose a children's literature selection to read aloud.

2. Read the book aloud to students, paying attention to both the textual cues and the illustrations.

3. When you have finished reading the book, ask the children what sounds they heard and have them identify if they were loud or soft.

4. Read the book with the children again. As they hear the sounds, ask them why they think they are loud or soft sounds. This second reading sparks their thinking for whether or not loud sounds could be heard in a quiet setting and vice versa.

Suggested Titles

Paul Bright, *Quiet!*

Margaret Wise Brown, *Sheep Don't Count Sheep*

Elizabeth Kimmel, *What Do You Dream?*

Jonathan London, *When the Fireflies Come*

Tony Mitton, *Goodnight Me, Goodnight You*

Mary O'Neill, *The Sound of Day, the Sound of Night*

Nancy Shaw, *Raccoon Tune*

Eileen Spinelli, *Rise the Moon*

Thomas Taylor, *The Loudest Roar*

Lisa Wheeler, *One Dark Night*

Deborah Wiles, *One Wide Sky*

Teacher Voice

As the school year began for second-grade teacher Jacque, she wanted her children to be more aware of the sounds around them. Understanding that this was a big task, she selected *The Sound of Day, the Sound of Night* to read to her class. As she read the book to her class, she made sure to read with expression as she came to the sound that each letter described. Understanding the importance of onomatopoeia, Jacque discussed with the children the sounds they heard. She then asked them to compare the sounds they heard—which were loud and which were soft? Jacque then told her students she would read the book to them again and reminded them of a new purpose for listening. She told them to listen for loud and soft sounds. She asked them to think about if they heard those sounds together or alone. Jacque also told her students to think about the sounds they hear throughout the day and how those sounds may affect them.

Extensions/Tips/Connections

1. Take a listening walk through a book such as *Rise the Moon* and ask children to listen for different sounds. Read through the book a second time. Have them discuss the sounds they hear as you read the story. Are the sounds loud or soft? Do they hear loud and soft sounds together or separately? This idea can be continued by taking an actual listening walk outside. Children can focus on either loud sounds or quiet sounds during their walk.

2. Read the book *Quiet!* with your class. As you read the book, have students identify if the scene described is a loud one or a quiet one. Throughout the book have them discuss what the lion's impact is on the story. Is he being loud or quiet? How will his behavior affect the scene? Help the students discriminate the sounds the lion makes and how those sounds might contrast with what the scene needs.

3. Picture Sounds: Read a book like *Raccoon Tune* to your class. As students listen to the story, have them determine if the sounds they hear are loud or soft. When asking the students why, have them explain their reasoning. Point out to the students that the illustration can help determine the sound of a book or a page as well. Softer colors emphasize softer voices. Likewise, a lot of things going on in the picture might show excitement and noise.

Hey now, what's that sound?

GRADE LEVEL: K-6

Description

One major writing device is creating a word that describes a sound, also known as *onomatopoeia*. This idea is a major component in discriminative listening. That is, children learn to discriminate among those words that describe specific sounds and those that do not. Hey Now, What's That Sound? is designed to help children recognize the important role these sounds play. Once adept at this aspect of listening, children can be encouraged to identify the sounds they think things make as well as create their own words to describe sounds they create.

Teaching Suggestions

1. Choose a children's literature selection that contains *onomatopoeia* to read loud.

2. Read the book aloud to the children.

3. When you finish the book, ask children what sounds were used and what words were used to describe the sounds. Then ask children to state the objects associated with the words.

4. Reread the book to the children, this time telling them to listen for when the sounds come in the story so they can join in when each sound occurs.

5. Remind the students that sounds play an important part in listening, and the sounds that things make can be an important idea to be aware of in their environments.

Suggested Titles

Leslie Baker, *The Animal ABC*

Susan Kuklin, *All Aboard! A True Train Story*

Michelle Meadows, *The Way the Storm Stops*

Chris Raschka, *Talk to Me About the Alphabet*

Tamson Weston, *Hey, Pancakes!*

Teacher Voice

First-grade teacher Mark noticed that every time he read aloud a book to his class the students did not pay much attention to what he was reading. They would listen for a few pages and then no longer engage with the story. Knowing that many students enjoyed trains, he chose to read *All Aboard! A True Train Story*. After reading the first few pages, he saw the students jump with surprise and excitement as they heard the words that describe the sounds that trains make during the story. After finishing the book, Mark asked his students what sounds were made in the book and what made those sounds. After a lively discussion, Mark invited his students to read the book with him, reminding them to listen for their part of the story. Mark had begun to teach his students that some words are used to better convey understanding of objects. He told his class, "When you're listening, this is something you can listen for."

Extensions/Tips/Connections

1. Onomatopoeia is not a concept just for younger students. Students in the intermediate grades can also work with sounds that objects make in a more complex way. The sizzle of pancakes on the griddle in the morning is the premise of *Hey, Pancakes!* Students can think of all the sounds objects make in their morning routines, from the beeping of an alarm clock, to the brushing of their teeth, to the slurping of milk while they eat their cereal. Students can work in pairs to come up with different sounds they experience each day. Another book that fits the needs of students from kindergarten through sixth grade is *Talk to Me About the Alphabet*.

2. Sound Effects: There are two different ideas that can be used with children that help them discriminate sounds they hear. One is to create a list of different objects that make noise. Looking at the list, invite students to write or say the sound they think each object makes. For the second idea, this activity can be reversed. The

students can listen to a tape that contains a number of different sounds and then write what they think makes each specific sound.

3. Creating the Sounds: Students enjoy dramatic activities, such as acting out a favorite story. To make the story more realistic, add sound effects. Children could then work together to create the sounds that are heard during a specific story. Again the children are working with onomatopoeia in a different light.

Show Me

GRADE LEVEL: K-6

Description

Discriminating listeners pay attention and assign meaning to the nonverbal cues provided by a speaker (Wolvin and Coakley 1996). A smile can mean that the speaker is enjoying the moment, whereas a frown can show displeasure. Hand and other body gestures also signal the listener about the speaker. Crossed arms can convey a closed attitude, whereas open arms convey just the opposite. One of the best ways to help children learn to interpret nonverbal cues is to provide them with some practice. Show Me is designed to do just that.

Teaching Suggestions

1. Select a picture book that contains detailed pictures of one or more characters.

2. Tell children that today you are going to begin reading the book by having them take a close look at the pictures. Also note that the reason you are asking them to do this is so that they will become better listeners by paying attention to the way individuals use their body language to convey a message.

3. As students look at the various pictures, invite them to share what they think each picture is trying to covey about the character. Does it show anger? Pleasure?

4. After providing children with this talk time, read the story.

5. Once the story is completed, provide children with time to tell whether or not their ideas were similar to the author's.

6. Remind children that paying attention to nonverbal cues is important both in and out of school. Nonverbal cues can be used to help listeners better understand the speaker.

Suggested Titles

Molly Bang, *Dawn*

Terry Farish, *The Cat Who Liked Potato Soup*

Jean Craighead George, *Frightful's Daughter*

Laurie Keller, *Arnie the Doughnut*

Rukhsana Khan, *Ruler of the Courtyard*

Walter Dean Myers, *Blues Journey*

Ernest L. Thayer, *Casey at the Bat*

Teacher Voice

As a result of watching her fifth graders interact with one another, Lois decided that a lesson in discriminative listening was in order. She wanted to show students how to pay attention to nonverbal cues so that students would better understand how to communicate with one another. She selected *Casey at the Bat* as a way to get the lesson going. Before showing the book to her students, Lois set the purpose by telling her students that much of what people use to understand a speaker cannot be heard, that they watch the speaker and get ideas based on how he uses his body. Paying attention to these nonverbal behaviors is important because they can help us to accurately interpret what the speaker is saying.

She then showed the students the pictures from the book and asked students to use the facial expressions and other nonverbal behaviors conveyed by the pictures of the story characters. Once students had an opportunity to talk about the book, Lois read the book. Finally, she had students note any likenesses and differences based on their initial interpretations and what they discovered as a result of listening to the story.

Extensions/Tips/Connections

1. Bring in a video or DVD that students have yet to see. Have children view part or all of it without the sound. Once the viewing is finished, invite children to tell about the nonverbal cues they used to get an idea about the characters. If time permits, have students take a second look but this time include the sound. Provide time to

discuss likenesses and differences among their initial interpretations, in which they used only nonverbal cues, and their second viewing.

2. Charades is an excellent game to help children learn about nonverbal cues. Players use the nonverbal cues to guess the word or words being acted out.

3. Children can be encouraged to use facial expressions to show different emotions. Others in class can use a nonverbal cue to discover the emotion best conveyed by that facial expression.

CHAPTER 2 TITLES

TONGUE-TYING TWISTERS

Andreae, Giles. 2002. *K Is for Kissing a Cool Kangaroo*. New York: Orchard.

Bauer, Marion Dane. 2003. *Why Do Kittens Purr?* New York: Simon and Schuster.

Brug, Sandra Gilbert. 2003. *Soccer Beat*. New York: Simon and Schuster (McElderry).

Cowley, Joy. 2003. *Mrs. Wishy-Washy's Farm*. New York: Philomel.

Dodds, Dayle Ann. 2003. *Where's Pup?* New York: Dial.

Fisher, Valorie. 2003. *Ellsworth's Extraordinary Electric Ears*. New York: Atheneum.

Isadora, Rachel. 2003. *Not Just Tutus*. New York: Putnam.

King, Stephen Michael. 2000. *Emily Loves to Bounce*. New York: Philomel.

Kolar, Bob. 2003. *Racer Dogs*. New York: Dutton.

Martin, Bill Jr. 2003. *Panda Bear, Panda Bear, What Do You See?* New York: Holt.

Mitton, Tony. 2002. *Dinosaurumpus!* New York: Orchard.

Polacco, Patricia. 2003. *G Is for Goat*. New York: Philomel.

Rose, Deborah Lee. 2003. *One Nighttime Sea*. New York: Scholastic.

HOW DO I FEEL?

Ashman, Linda. 2003. *Rub-a-Dub-Dub*. San Diego: Harcourt.

Florczak, Robert. 2003. *Yikes!!!* New York: Scholastic.

Frazee, Marla. 2003. *Roller Coaster*. San Diego: Harcourt.

Johnston, Tony. 2003. *Go Track a Yak*. New York: Simon and Schuster.

Khan, Rukhsana. 2003. *Ruler of the Courtyard*. New York: Viking.

Krosoczka, Jarrett. 2003. *Bubble Bath Pirates!* New York: Viking.

Schotter, Roni. 2003. *Captain Bob Takes Flight*. New York: Atheneum.

Thompson, Pat. 2003. *Drat That Fat Cat*. New York: Scholastic.

Wheeler, Lisa. 2003. *One Dark Night*. San Diego: Harcourt.

Wilson, Karma. 2003. *Bear Wants More*. New York: Simon and Schuster (McElderry).

LOUD OR SOFT SOUNDS?

Bright, Paul. 2003. *Quiet!* New York: Orchard.

Brown, Margaret Wise. 2003. *Sheep Don't Count Sheep*. New York: Simon and Schuster (McElderry).

Kimmel, Elizabeth. 2003. *What Do You Dream?* Cambridge, MA: Candlewick.

London, Jonathan. 2003. *When the Fireflies Come*. New York: Dutton.

Mitton, Tony. 2002. *Goodnight Me, Goodnight You*. New York: Little, Brown.

O'Neill, Mary. 1966. *The Sound of Day, the Sound of Night*. New York: Farrar, Straus and Giroux.

Shaw, Nancy. 2003. *Raccoon Tune*. New York: Holt.

Spinelli, Eileen. 2003. *Rise the Moon*. New York: Dial.

Taylor, Thomas. 2002. *The Loudest Roar*. New York: Scholastic.

Wiles, Deborah. 2003. *One Wide Sky*. San Diego: Harcourt.

HEY NOW, WHAT'S THAT SOUND?

Baker, Leslie. 2003. *The Animal ABC*. New York: Holt.

Kuklin, Susan. 2003. *All Aboard! A True Train Story*. New York: Orchard.

Meadows, Michelle. 2003. *The Way the Storm Stops*. New York: Holt.

Raschka, Chris. 2003. *Talk to Me About the Alphabet*. New York: Holt.

Weston, Tamson. 2003. *Hey, Pancakes!* San Diego: Harcourt.

SHOW ME

Bang, Molly. 2002. *Dawn*. New York: SeaStar.

Farish, Terry. 2003. *The Cat Who Liked Potato Soup*. Cambridge, MA: Candlewick.

George, Jean Craighead. 2002. *Frightful's Daughter*. New York: Dutton.

Keller, Laurie. 2003. *Arnie the Doughnut*. New York: Henry Holt.

Khan, Rukhsana. 2003. *Ruler of the Courtyard*. New York: Viking.

Myers, Walter Dean. 2003. *Blues Journey*. New York: Holiday House.

Thayer, Ernest L. 2003. *Casey at the Bat*. New York: Simon and Schuster.

3

Precise Listening

"They just don't pay attention."

"They don't seem to get the details of what I'm telling them."

Comments such as these show that we as teachers are aware and concerned about listening. In this instance, what we want seems easy: "Just listen to what I say and get the facts. All you have to do is pay attention." Seems simple enough, but there is quite a difference between expecting students to listen and showing them how.

Precise listening, or "accurate listening" (Devine 1982), is listening that requires students to pay attention and to ascertain details of a talk. It builds on discriminative listening (see Chapter 2). DeHaven (1989) lists these skills as sample skills associated with precise listening: associating words and meanings, deducing the meaning of unknown words from context, understanding grammatical structures, forming sensory impressions, recalling details, recalling sequences, and paraphrasing information (p. 74).

In order for children to be precise listeners, we need to go beyond telling to showing. Fortunately for the children we teach, there are ways that we can do so. This chapter provides five suggestions. For instance, Give Me Five (pp. 37–41) is designed to provide students with a framework for grasping specific details from a talk or video. Figure 3–1 provides an overview of this strategy and four additional teaching suggestions and the listening skills each develops.

Regardless of the strategy, however, Devine (1982) offers these general suggestions to ensure effective teaching of precise listening:

SKILL	GIVE ME FIVE	WHAT'S THE GOOD WORD?	TALK SHOW	ADD ONE	ARE YOU FOLLOWING?
Associating words and meanings		•			
Deducing the meaning of unknown words from context		•			
Understanding grammatical structures		•			•
Forming sensory impressions			•	•	
Recalling details	•		•	•	
Recalling sequences	•		•	•	
Paraphrasing information	•		•	•	
Following directions					•
Recognizing multiple characters			•	•	

3–1.

Effective Precise-Listening Teaching Strategies and the Skills They Develop

1. *Build the lessons into the daily and weekly schedules.* Doing so underscores for students that they need to be more precise in their listening on an ongoing basis. More frequent lessons of shorter duration have a more lasting impact than longer less frequent lessons.

2. *Emphasize good listening behavior.* Believe it or not, some students have little understanding of good listening manners even though they may have been told to "be quiet." They need to be reminded of and shown good listening behaviors, such as

   - looking at the speaker

   - remaining quiet when another is speaking

   - thinking about what the speaker is saying

3. *Provide a good role model.* One of the best ways for students to learn how to attend to others is to see their teacher model appropriate behaviors. When they talk to us, we focus on them rather than some other task. We use nonverbal cues such as nodding the head to show that we are comprehending.

4. *Make lessons a part of ongoing instruction.* As noted earlier (see Chapter 1), integrating listening lessons with other lessons helps students see that listening is anything but a one-time event that happens at a given time of day. Rather, listening is used throughout the day.

GIVE ME FIVE

GRADE LEVEL: 1-6

Description

Precise listening invites listening for specific information such as the main point a speaker is trying to make or the details associated with it. What is most important is that the listener understands the purpose for listening at the onset. Providing students with some sort of listening guide is one way to establish a purpose for listening and provide concrete evidence that the listener did indeed accomplish the purpose. Using Give Me Five, you tell students what to listen for and provide a structured guide on which students can make note of their discoveries.

Teaching Suggestions

1. Choose a children's literature selection that highlights the specific skill you are trying to help students learn. For example, if you want students to listen for details, work with a selection that has several details.

2. Construct a listening guide that can be used by children to make notes. Figure 3–2 shows one example.

3. Show the book and the listening guide to the students.

4. Explain to children the purpose for listening to the read-aloud and how you want them to complete the listening guide. Make sure students understand that they are to listen for at least five details and write each in the appropriate space on the guide. Once they have five details, they can write additional details in the space provided.

5. Distribute the listening guide and read the book.

6. Have children fill in their listening guides as you read the book.

Give Me Five

Name: _____

Title of Book: _____

Five Details I Heard:

1. _____

2. _____

3. _____

4. _____

5. _____

Other Details:

3–2.

7. After reading the book, review the listening guide with the children and provide them with some time to give you and their classmates five details they were able to glean from the listening experience. You can invite students to listen to the details their classmates share and note likenesses and differences among them.

Suggested Titles

Mary M. Cerullo, *Sea Turtles: Ocean Nomads*

Lynne Cherry, *How Groundhog's Garden Grew*

Lynn Curlee, *Capital*

Nicola Davies, *Surprising Sharks*

Allan Drummond, *The Flyers*

Denise Fleming, *Buster*

Cheryl Harness, *Rabble Rousers: Twenty Women Who Made a Difference*

Bruce Hiscock, *The Big Caribou Herd*

Kathryn Lasky, *The Man Who Made Time Travel*

Jim Mastro, *Antarctic Ice*

Penelope Niven, *Carl Sandburg: Adventures of a Poet*

Amy Schwartz, *What James Likes Best*

Richard Sobol, *Adelina's Whales*

Stephen R. Swinburne, *Black Bear: North America's Bear*

Ruth Symes, *The Sheep Fairy: When Wishes Have Dreams*

Jean Van Leeuwen, *The Amazing Air Balloon*

Teacher Voice

Doug wanted his fifth-grade students to become better at listening for details while simultaneously learning how to construct a historical time line. He decided to use *Carl Sandburg: Adventures of a Poet* because of the many details it provides about Sandburg's life as well as some of his poetry. What's more, when reviewing the book, Doug noticed that it included a time line that showed the major events in Sandburg's life juxtaposed with historical events. The time line was connected with train tracks marked with the years in which the events occurred. He saw this as a perfect listening guide. He drew train tracks down the middle of a blank page. On each railroad tie, he wrote the appropriate year(s), leaving spaces on either side for students to write associated details (see Figure 3–3). Once prepared, Doug then told students how to use the guide: "One of the most important skills you need to learn is

Follow the Track

CARL SANDBURG'S LIFE: HISTORICAL DETAILS:

Details   Years

Details   Years

Details   Years

Details   Years

Details   Years

3–3.

Doug's Listening Guide

how to listen for details. That is going to be the focus of today's lesson." He then went on to explain how to use the listening guide, saying, "While I am reading the book, you need to listen for at least one detail that tells about Sandburg's life and one that tells about a historical event for each of the years shown on your train track. You then need to write these sentences in your guide." Finally, he began reading the book, stopping occasionally to give students time to write what they heard about the given years shown on the train track. Once he finished reading, he showed students the time line in the book. Students compared their guides with the one in the book. Doug closed the lesson by reminding students how they could use this type of listening in their everyday lives. "So the next time you want to get specific information from someone who is talking to you, think first about what it is you want to know and then make notes so that you can remember what you heard."

Extensions/Tips/Connections

1. Rather than making a guide for students, you might want them to construct their own. For example, to prepare our college students for a video view, we often have them fold a piece of paper into sections and label each. As students watch the video, they write pertinent information in each section. We also encourage them to paraphrase so that they can remain focused on the basic ideas shown in the video rather than on specific words. Once the video is finished, students share what they gleaned with one another, filling in details as needed.

2. Make It Fast is a variation of the listening guide (Wolvin and Coakley 1979). Students are expected to listen to a taped, detailed speech for ten minutes. Students write all the details they can remember and then compare their notes with those details mentioned in the speech. As students become better able to comprehend the message, the speed and/or length of the speech can be increased.

3. To help students determine a specific sequence of events, after reading aloud a book such as *Buster*, give students sentence strips that show specific events from the story and ask them to sequence the events. Once they have sequenced all the events, students can cross-check with the book to determine how accurate they were.

What's the Good Word?

GRADE LEVEL: K-6

Description

One way that children learn words is by hearing them in meaningful contexts (Elley 1989). Story reading is one such context. Through stories, children are exposed to words representative of different languages as well as to new words and words with multiple meanings. Through listening, children need only attend to the meanings of words; decoding is not necessary. The main focus is on expanding children's listening vocabulary so that they can better understand speakers. This expanded listening vocabulary also makes reading easier. That is, it is much easier to read words we have heard. In this activity, students are invited to listen to a story or passage to identify and determine word meanings from context.

Teaching Suggestions

1. Choose an appropriate children's literature selection such as *Oh No, Gotta Go!* Texts that have idioms or words with multiple meanings work well.

2. Provide students with some background for the text.

3. Let students know that there may be some words that are new to them but if they listen carefully, they will be able to understand them by using the words that come before and after them.

4. Read the book aloud to the students and have them listen for new words.

5. After reading the story a second time, ask volunteers to tell new words that they heard and what they think they mean.

6. As students share words, revisit the pages where they appear and reread the pages or sentences to verify both the words and their meanings.

Suggested Titles

Kathi Appelt, *Piggies in a Polka*

Peter Cohen, *Boris's Glasses*

Susan Middleton Elya, *Eight Animals Play Ball*

Susan Middleton Elya, *Oh No, Gotta Go!*

Loreen Leedy and Pat Street, *There's a Frog in My Throat!*

Peter Glassman, *My Dad's Job*

June Sobel, *B Is for Bulldozer: A Construction ABC*

Alexander Stadler, *Beverly Billingsly Takes a Bow*

Teacher Voice

Kayla teaches in a bilingual school in which children learn both English and Spanish. She immerses her second graders with Spanish as much as possible throughout the day. Her student observations have confirmed her belief that children best learn words by hearing them in authentic settings. To help children broaden their listening vocabularies of Spanish words, she selected *Oh No, Gotta Go!* to read aloud. She set the stage before reading by holding up the book and asking students to look closely at the cover to see if they recognized anything out of the ordinary. More than one student noted that there were English words and Spanish words on the cover. Kayla then told students that this book had several Spanish words that they might not know. She also told them that if they listened carefully to the rest of the words on the pages, however, they would be able to understand the Spanish words. She then proceeded to read aloud. During a second reading, Kayla stopped at each bold-print word and asked students, "What's the good word?" Kayla closed the lesson by telling students that one of the best ways to learn a new word is to listen to how the word is used in the sentence or story. Paying attention to the meanings of words better ensures that the listener will understand what the speaker is trying to communicate.

Extensions/Tips/Connections

1. Rost (1991) offers an alternative to this activity that calls for students to focus on the grammatical structures as well as the words.

He suggests providing students with two oral versions of a given text, one of which has been slightly altered. Students listen to both texts and note differences.

2. One way to focus students' attention on the meaning of idioms is to read a book such as *My Dad's Job*. Children can listen to determine the literal meaning of the idioms. Children can then select an idiom from a book such as *There's a Frog in My Throat!* and illustrate it. Then you can post these illustrations on a bulletin board titled "What's the Good Word?" In this way, the bulletin board acts as a riddle for children to determine the meanings of the various idioms.

3. To explore multiple meanings of words, invite children to create and share their own sentences with one another. After reading a sentence aloud, the student asks, "What's the good word?" and calls on volunteers to tell what they think the word means.

TALK SHOW

GRADE LEVEL: K-6

Description

In literature children meet many characters. For some children it is challenging to distinguish specific attributes for each character. Talk Show is an activity that encourages children to listen carefully to the story so they can determine what the characters are like. This activity shows that children are already able to discriminate the voices they hear as different characters in the book. Talk Show goes beyond discriminative listening. Students are able to identify specific characteristics of the characters they meet in the story based upon their listening.

Teaching Suggestions

1. Choose a children's literature selection to read aloud (e.g., one that contains well-known characters from other stories that children recognize).

2. Tell the children the purpose of the read-aloud is to listen closely to the descriptions of what specific characters in the book are like.

3. Read the book aloud to the children.

4. After reading the book, discuss with the children what specific characteristics they feel the characters have.

5. Invite children to become the characters on a talk show. As the teacher, you will be the host of the talk show. (Later, the students can be the host(s).) Ask questions that allow the children to become the characters based upon what they heard from the book or could infer from the book.

Suggested Titles

Bonny Becker, *An Ant's Day Off*

Candace Fleming, *Boxes for Katje*

Michael Garland, *Miss Smith's Incredible Storybook*

Joan Sandin, *Coyote School News*

Andrea U'Ren, *Mary Smith*

Teacher Voice

Fourth-grade teacher Charlie decided he wanted his students to listen for the specific attributes of the characters from the books he read aloud to his class. Since Charlie already read with great expression, he knew his students were able to distinguish the different characters in the stories. Charlie now wanted them to describe their own characteristics for each character, based upon their listening. Charlie read *Miss Smith's Incredible Storybook* to his class. When he finished reading, he asked his students what different characters came out from Miss Smith's storybook. He then asked the students what they thought certain characters were like. After a brief discussion he invited seven students to become guests on the *Mr. McCarthy Talk Show*. His guests were different characters that came alive from the storybook as well as Miss Smith, Zack, and Principal Rittenrotten. Through the talk show, Charlie was able to provide his students the opportunity to show how their listening enabled them to become characters from the book. Charlie also reinforced the importance that nonverbal cues can play when listening to someone talk.

Extensions/Tips/Connections

1. Stories come in different forms. *Coyote School News* tells a story in newspaper format about a school and all the activities the different classes are doing. Teachers can invite children to take on the multiple roles that are used in creating a newspaper. The students can listen like a reporter getting ready to write a story. They could also listen as an editor would, or even as a reader of the newspaper. This activity helps children begin to understand the importance of listening before they begin writing.

2. People hear different messages. Often children all hear something but get an entirely different message from what is being said. *An Ant's Day Off* allows children to hear what happens to one ant when he decides he needs a day off. Children also are able to hear other characters' descriptions of what happens in their day. At the

end of the book learners can discuss what different things happened to the characters as well as what taking a day off might mean to the different characters.

3. What Do You Need? The story in *Boxes for Katje* is written through letter correspondence between characters in America and Holland. Students can listen to each letter and predict what they think could be sent to the pen pal in response. As the care packages get bigger, students' predictions can also become more involved. This is an excellent example of a book that could be used for interactive read-alouds, in which students become involved in the book *while* you are reading it.

ADD ONE

GRADE LEVEL: K-6

Description

Children listen to a number of stories every day. Whether they are from their friends, relatives, or teachers, telling stories is a common feature in every child's life. In order to comprehend the story, children need to be able to listen and understand what they are being told. Add One asks children to listen to a fun story and understand specific aspects of the story that appeal to them. This activity encourages children to listen to specific details in a story and share them with their classmates.

Teaching Suggestions

1. Choose a children's literature selection to read aloud that has one main character telling a story.

2. Tell the children to listen carefully for the story that is being told.

3. Read the story aloud.

4. Discuss with the students what the story was about. Have individuals share one detail they heard from the story. After one student has shared a detail, have the next student say the first detail and then add one more. Continue this process until the class has tapped all the details.

5. Remind the students that *everyone* has a story to tell. Also remind them that listening can be highly personal—we focus on specific details based on our previous experiences and interests.

Suggested Titles

Pat Brisson, *Star Blanket*

Ashley Bryan, *Beautiful Blackbird*

Eric Carle, *Where Are You Going? To See My Friend!*

Alexis Deacon, *Beegu*

Baba Wague Diakite, *The Magic Gourd*

Cristine King Farris, *My Brother Martin*

Kathryn Lasky, *Before I Was Your Mother*

Melinda Long, *How I Became a Pirate*

Robert Munsch, *Lighthouse: A Story of Remembrance*

Leslea Newman, *Pigs, Pigs, Pigs*

Diana Reynolds Roome, *The Elephant's Pillow*

Robert D. San Souci, *Little Pierre: A Cajun Story from Louisiana*

Aaron Shepard, *The Princess Mouse*

Janet Stevens and Susan Stevens Crummel, *Jackalope*

Lisa Wheeler, *Avalanche Annie: A Not-So-Tall Tale*

Teacher Voice

Peter is a third-grade teacher who would like his students to be able to recall specific information from a story. He decides to try an activity called Add One. Peter picks *How I Became a Pirate* to read to his class. Before he reads, he tells his students to pay attention to details in the story. Peter uses the pirate theme in the book to read with expression and uses pirate voices throughout the book. After reading the story to the class, he asks for someone to share one detail from the book. A child shares a detail, and Peter asks for another. He has the second child restate the first detail and then add one more detail. Peter continues to have his children add one detail until they have shared all the details. Peter concludes this lesson by reminding his students that every story contains many details and that connecting details helps listeners understand what's being shared with them, whether it's a story, instructions, or new information.

Extensions/Tips/Connections

1. New Stories: Books such as *My Brother Martin* are a good way to have students learn about new stories with characters they may already know. *My Brother Martin* is the story of Martin Luther King Jr. and his childhood, told by his sister. Children can use what they already know about Martin Luther King Jr. and add any new information from the book. Doing so allows children to compare the new details to the knowledge they already had about the subject.

2. Add One, Continued: The idea of Add One can also be used to extend children's thinking when they are writing. Take a basic sentence such as "It is snowing." Have children work individually or in pairs to add on to the sentence. Have them add on the who, what, where, when, and how to the sentences. Then have them illustrate the sentences and display them in the classroom. Children will have a fun way to learn the importance of details. This activity can also be completed in a large-group setting.

3. Detail Web: Many books, such as *Beegu*, allow children the opportunity to work with details. After reading the book to children create a detail web. Using the main character as the center of the web, draw the details as extensions of the web. Students listen to their classmates' ideas as the web continues to grow. If you record the web on chart paper, you can post it in the room so students have a good reference for using details in their listening, not to mention reading and writing.

ARE YOU FOLLOWING?

GRADE LEVEL: K-6

Description

Following directions is a skill we must use both in and out of school. And many times, we are expected to follow directions by simply listening. Just the other day, for example, a friend of mine (Michael) was explaining to me how to play a sport called squash. Successful playing of the game relied, in part, on my being able to listen to the directions. Often oral directions are quite involved, such as when someone is trying to explain how to play a card game. Clearly, listening to elaborate directions and following them in order to successfully complete a task is a learned behavior. We can make the task easier if we begin by giving simple directions with an eye on increasing the level of difficulty once students have proved successful with following simple directions.

Teaching Suggestions

1. Select a passage or a book to read aloud to children that involves following directions in order to complete a task.

2. Explain to students that the purpose for listening to the book is to help them learn how to listen to and follow directions.

3. Ask students why they think that being able to follow stated directions is important.

4. Read the book to the students.

5. On a second reading of the book, have children identify the directions that the character was to follow and whether or not he or she followed them.

Suggested Titles

Martha Alexander, *I'll Never Share You, Blackboard Bear*

Jim Arnosky, *Armadillo's Orange*

Emma Chichester Clark, *Follow the Leader!*

Margaret A. Hartelius, *Knot Now! The Complete Friendship Bracelet Kit!*

Anastasia Suen, *Raise the Roof!*

Christine Widman, *Cornfield Hide-and-Seek*

Teacher Voice

Michael wanted to provide his first graders with some practice in following oral directions. Teaching first graders for several years had shown him that being able to follow oral directions is a learned behavior that happens over time. He selected *Armadillo's Orange* as a way to help students learn this most important skill. After talking with his students about why following directions is important both in and out of school, Michael told his students that learning how to follow directions takes some practice, which was exactly the purpose of that day's reading. He asked students to listen for how the armadillo remembers where his burrow is. He then proceeded to read the book for sheer enjoyment. When finished, he asked his students, "So how did the armadillo find his way home?" and provided time for them to share their thoughts. On a second reading of the book, Michael asked his students to stop him every time they heard a direction given to the armadillo. He wrote these directions on a piece of chart paper for all to see. When he finished reading, Michael reviewed the chart with the class. He closed the lesson by reminding students that being able to listen to and follow oral directions is important both in and out of school. Like the armadillo learned, being able to follow directions is often a matter of safety.

Extensions/Tips/Connections

1. One way to help students extend their ability to follow several directions is to play some sort of listening game. For example, when dismissing students for the day, give students several directions, such as "Stand up. Put your chair on top of your desk. Walk to the closet and get your belongings. Walk to your mailbox and get your papers. Stand in line." Choose a student to complete these directions while the rest of the class watches to see if she completes them in the order given.

2. Have each student make a simple drawing. Next, pair students, placing some sort of screen between them. One person takes on the role of explainer and the other is the listener. The explainer tells the listener how to construct the image that is on his page. When the pair decide they have completed the task, they can lift the screen and compare their drawings. The two drawings should match if the explainer clearly stated the directions and the listener followed them closely.

3. What Are You Making? Have students explain how to make something and have others do just what they say. For example, students can tell one another how to make a peanut butter sandwich. Have the listeners follow the directions as stated. Students could also listen to the directions and guess what the speaker is making.

GIVE ME FIVE

Cerullo, Mary M. 2003. *Sea Turtles: Ocean Nomads*. New York: Dutton.

Cherry, Lynne. 2003. *How Groundhog's Garden Grew*. New York: Scholastic.

Curlee, Lynn. 2003. *Capital*. New York: Atheneum.

Davies, Nicola. 2003. *Surprising Sharks*. Cambridge, MA: Candlewick.

Drummond, Allan. 2003. *The Flyers*. New York: Farrar, Straus, and Giroux.

Fleming, Denise. 2003. *Buster*. New York: Henry Holt.

Harness, Cheryl. 2003. *Rabble Rousers: Twenty Women Who Made a Difference*. New York: Dutton.

Hiscock, Bruce. 2003. *The Big Caribou Herd*. Honesdale, PA: Boyds Mills.

Lasky, Kathryn. 2003. *The Man Who Made Time Travel*. New York: Farrar, Straus, and Giroux.

Mastro, Jim. 2003. *Antarctic Ice*. New York: Henry Holt.

Niven, Penelope. 2003. *Carl Sandburg: Adventures of a Poet*. San Diego: Harcourt.

Schwartz, Amy. 2003. *What James Likes Best*. New York: Atheneum.

Sobol, Richard. 2003. *Adelina's Whales*. New York: Dutton.

Swinburne, Stephen R. 2003. *Black Bear: North America's Bear*. Honesdale, PA: Boyds Mills.

Symes, Ruth. 2003. *The Sheep Fairy: When Wishes Have Dreams*. New York: Scholastic.

Van Leeuwen, Jean. 2003. *The Amazing Air Balloon*. New York: Putnam.

WHAT'S THE GOOD WORD?

Appelt, Kathi. 2003. *Piggies in a Polka*. San Diego: Harcourt.

Cohen, Peter. *Boris's Glasses*. New York: Farrar, Straus, and Giroux.

Elya, Susan Middleton. 2003. *Eight Animals Play Ball*. New York: Putnam.

————. 2003. *Oh No, Gotta Go!* New York: Putnam.

Glassman, Peter. 2003. *My Dad's Job*. New York: Simon and Schuster.

Leedy, Loreen, and Pat Street. 2003. *There's a Frog in My Throat!* New York: Holiday House.

Sobel, June. 2003. *B Is for Bulldozer: A Construction ABC*. San Diego: Harcourt.

Stadler, Alexander. 2003. *Beverly Billingsly Takes a Bow*. San Diego: Harcourt.

TALK SHOW

Becker, Bonny. 2003. *An Ant's Day Off*. New York: Simon and Schuster.

Fleming, Candace. 2003. *Boxes for Katje*. New York: Farrar, Straus, and Giroux.

Garland, Michael. 2003. *Miss Smith's Incredible Storybook*. New York: Dutton.

Sandin, Joan. 2003. *Coyote School News*. New York: Henry Holt.

U'Ren, Andrea. 2003. *Mary Smith*. New York: Farrar, Straus, and Giroux.

ADD ONE

Brisson, Pat. 2003. *Star Blanket*. Honesdale, PA: Boyds Mills.

Bryan, Ashley. 2003. *Beautiful Blackbird*. New York: Atheneum.

Carle, Eric. 2001. *Where Are You Going? To See My Friend!* New York: Orchard.

Deacon, Alexis. 2003. *Beegu*. New York: Farrar, Straus, and Giroux.

Diakite, Baba Wague. 2003. *The Magic Gourd*. New York: Scholastic.

Farris, Cristine King. 2003. *My Brother Martin*. New York: Simon and Schuster.

Lasky, Kathryn. 2003. *Before I Was Your Mother*. San Diego: Harcourt.

Long, Melinda. 2003. *How I Became a Pirate*. San Diego: Harcourt.

Munsch, Robert. 2003. *Lighthouse: A Story of Remembrance*. New York: Scholastic.

Newman, Leslea. 2003. *Pigs, Pigs, Pigs*. New York: Simon and Schuster.

Roome, Diana Reynolds. 2003. *The Elephant's Pillow*. New York: Farrar, Straus, and Giroux.

San Souci, Robert D. 2003. *Little Pierre: A Cajun Story from Louisiana*. San Diego: Harcourt.

Shepard, Aaron. 2003. *The Princess Mouse*. New York: Atheneum.

Stevens, Janet, and Susan Stevens Crummel. 2003. *Jackalope*. San Diego: Harcourt.

Wheeler, Lisa. 2003. *Avalanche Annie: A Not-So-Tall Tale*. San Diego: Harcourt.

ARE YOU FOLLOWING?

Alexander, Martha. 2003. *I'll Never Share You, Blackboard Bear*. Cambridge, MA: Candlewick.

Arnosky, Jim. 2003. *Armadillo's Orange*. New York: Putnam.

Clark, Emma Chichester. 2003. *Follow the Leader!* New York: McElderry.

Hartelius, Margaret A. 2003. *Knot Now! The Complete Friendship Bracelet Kit!* New York: Putnam.

Suen, Anastasia. 2003. *Raise the Roof!* New York: Viking.

Widman, Christine. 2003. *Cornfield Hide-and-Seek*. New York: Farrar, Straus, and Giroux.

4

Strategic Listening

A teacher in one of my (Michael) graduate courses said it best. As a result of doing some research on listening, she concluded, "I knew that hearing and listening were not the same; I sensed when my students were not understanding what I felt they needed to learn from oral presentations, but I was uncertain about how to support them appropriately. Now I have some ideas."

As this quote illustrates, one of the main reasons we listen is to understand the speaker's intended message. Much can interfere with this process, as we noted in Chapter 1. Oftentimes, students need to be taught how to listen to gain understanding. They need to be taught how to identify when comprehension is breaking down and what to do about it. Connecting ideas and new information, connecting prior knowledge with new information, summarizing, comparing and contrasting, and making inferences are the kinds of cognitive strategies students are called on to use when they listen to understand a message. There is ample evidence that these strategies can indeed be taught (Imhof 2000; Lundsteen 1979).

Sometimes called "listening for understanding" (DeHaven 1989) or "comprehensive listening" (Wolvin and Coakley 1996), strategic listening helps children develop these cognitive and metacognitive abilities. This level of listening calls on the listener to concentrate on the intended meaning of the speaker's message in order to best understand it. It asks the listener to set aside all analysis and judgments of the message. Successful strategic listeners are those who can understand the message and remember it for the future.

This chapter offers a variety of teaching strategies to help children develop strategic listening. Fill in the Gaps (pp. 59–62), for example, helps children learn how make inferences while listening, whereas the Directed Listening-Thinking Activity (pp. 63–65) shows students how to monitor their listening throughout a speaking event. Figure 4–1 shows the strategies each activity in this chapter emphasizes.

SKILL	FILL IN THE GAPS	DIRECTED LISTENING-THINKING ACTIVITY	STRUCTURED LISTENING ACTIVITY	SUM IT UP!	GET THE PICTURE
Connecting ideas and information	•	•		•	
Connecting prior knowledge with new information	•	•		•	•
Summarizing				•	
Predicting		•			•
Questioning			•		
Inferencing	•				
Distinguishing between inferences and factual information	•			•	
Identifying implied main ideas				•	
Classifying and organizing information that supports a main idea				•	•

4-1.

Effective Strategic-Listening Teaching Strategies and the Skills They Develop

FILL IN THE GAPS
Making Inferences

GRADE LEVEL: K-6

Description

Making inferences is a comprehension strategy that we continually use. Knowing how to make inferences is important because the listener can then make some decisions about what is being shared. Is the speaker stating some information but expecting the listener to fill in the gaps to arrive at an understanding of the message? Answering this question provides the listeners with a reason to listen. Listeners are set up to do some thinking on their own as the speaker shares her message. According to Alverman (1984), using a listening comprehension guide is an effective way to teach children *how* to make inferences rather than just *telling* them to do so. That is, it explicitly shows children how to interact with the spoken message. Assuming that different types of texts are used with the listening guide, children can learn to make inferences from a wide variety of texts. And as noted in Chapter 3, children can totally focus on using listening because decoding text is not necessary. Teaching students listening strategies tends to improve their listening comprehension. Alverman notes that this is especially true if the listening skills relate to reading, children are actively involved in follow-up activities, and literature is used. The listening guide described here meets all three criteria.

Teaching Suggestions

(These are based on Alverman [1984].)

1. Choose a text that encourages inference making.

2. Construct a listening guide, keeping it simple to start. This guide is for teacher use. Use declarative statements that represent different

levels of comprehension: literal, interpretive, and applied. When reading the text, insert at least three stopping points, each representing a different level of comprehension. The *literal level* demands that students focus on what is actually stated in the text. At the *interpretive level*, students are more actively involved in inferring because they have to reason beyond what is directly stated in the text. At the *applied level*, students talk about how the story or an event from the story relates to their lives.

3. Set the purpose for the whole listening experience by stating no more than three declarative statements related to the text.

4. Read the entire book.

5. Revisit the statements that you made prior to reading the book. Provide time for student responses.

6. Next, provide students with statements at the interpretive level and provide time for discussion.

7. Provide students with statements at the applied level and provide time for discusssion.

8. Remind students of why listening and making inferences is important.

Suggested Titles

Paul Owen Lewis, *The Jupiter Stone*

Marilyn Singer, *Fireflies at Midnight*

Audrey Wood, *Alphabet Mystery*

Wong Herbert Yee, *Tracks in the Snow*

Teacher Voice

To help her first graders learn to make inferences while simultaneously learning more about the alphabet, Nancy selected *Alphabet Mystery* and constructed a listening guide. Before reading the book to the children, she commented, "The book I am going to read to you today is *Alphabet Mystery*, by Audrey Wood. These are some ideas the author tells you about Charley's alphabet:

1. All of the letters from Charley's alphabet go to bed every night.

2. Charley's alphabet has to search for one missing letter.

3. Charley's alphabet letters work together to make a birthday cake.

"Please listen to the story. If I come to a part that tells that Charley's alphabet goes to bed every night, the alphabet has to search for one missing letter, or the alphabet letters work together to make a birthday cake, please raise your hand."

She then read the story and noted when children raised their hands. After reading, she commented, "You did an excellent job of listening to what the author said about Charley's alphabet. Now I want you to pretend that you are detectives and tell how the alphabet was able to get 'little x' to return home. Just like detectives use clues to solve their problems, I want you to tell me what clues you used from the story to tell how the alphabet was able to get 'little x' to come home." She provided time for students to share their ideas and clues. Finally, she told her students, "You have shown that you can do two things when you listen to a story. You showed that you could listen to exactly what the author stated. You also showed that you can put the pieces together to understand what the author wanted you to understand even though she didn't exactly tell you. Now I want you to show how you can use what you already know to help you understand what 'little x' was feeling. Listen as I read this sentence: 'I ran away because Charley never uses me.' Think about a time when you felt that you weren't appreciated. Tell how your feelings are like those of 'little x.'" After students shared their ideas, Nancy closed the lesson by telling her students that sometimes listeners have to think very carefully about what the author is saying to best understand a story. Knowing how to listen for what is stated and what the author wants you to understand is important because it helps you understand the story better. Comparing something in your life with an event from the story is one way to better remember the story. It also makes listening more enjoyable.

Extensions/Tips/Connections

1. Remember that the guide described here is extremely flexible. You might want to begin with the applied level, then move to the literal level, and end with the interpretive level. Also, depending on the students (i.e., their ages and abilities), you can work toward eliminating specific statements to guide the listening. You can use generic questions to prompt children to talk about the text.

2. A variation of this listening guide is to read some statements that are either true or partially true to students prior to reading the story. Tell students that they are to listen to the story to determine which of the statements are true and those that are partially true. After reading the story, revisit each statement and provide time for students to share their ideas. You can encourage students to use the text to verify clues that led them to respond as they did.

3. Using a book such as *The Jupiter Stone*, invite children to fill in gaps between what is told in the story and what the listener needs to infer. For example, in the book the stone lands and millions of years pass. Children can fill in the gaps by talking about what might happen to the rock over time. How might it look? How does it move closer to the water?

DIRECTED LISTENING-THINKING ACTIVITY (DLTA)
Making Predictions

GRADE LEVEL: K-6

Description

Making predictions is one important comprehension strategy. It requires students to use past experiences in combination with the new information about a selection or talk to make logical guesses (i.e., predictions) about the content of the story or the talk. After making predictions, students then listen to confirm or change their predictions based on what they hear. The Directed Listening-Thinking Activity is one way to help students learn to make predictions. Discussion occurs before, during, and after the story or talk to help students better understand how to make and monitor predictions throughout. One of the major goals is to help students understand that making predictions is ongoing rather than a one-time event. Another goal is to help students see that making predictions is one way to stay involved in the story or talk, making understanding of either more likely.

Teaching Suggestions

(These are based on on Rubin [2000].)

1. Prepare for the presentation, which can take on many forms such as reading a story, presenting a talk, playing an audiotape or a CD, or playing a video or DVD. To best prepare, relate the current presentation with listeners' past experiences, provide an overview, present any unique vocabulary, and pose questions at different difficulty levels.

2. Share with students that the purpose for listening is to help them learn more about making and using predictions.

3. Read the story or make the presentation as the students listen for answers for some of the questions you posed earlier.

4. Stop at various points and ask students whether or not they have answers to any of the questions. At this point ask some additional questions to guide students' listening.

5. Read to the next stopping point and, once again, discuss any answers to questions you posed and make new predictions.

6. After the story or presentation is finished, provide time for children to answer any unanswered questions. You can also ask additional challenging questions. Then ask students to state the central idea of the talk and give a short summary of it.

7. As an optional step, invite students to create some questions that could be used in subsequent readings of the text.

8. Remind students that making predictions is important because it can help them stay focused on the message the speaker is trying to communicate. Making predictions and listening to confirm or modify them is also a way to stay actively involved with the story or the talk.

Suggested Titles

Arthur Howard, *Serious Trouble*

Satomi Ichikawa, *My Pig Amarillo*

Ernst Jandl, *Next Please*

Meghan McCarthy, *George Upside Down*

Nancy Minchella, *Mama Will Be Home Soon*

Julia Noonan, *Mouse by Mouse: A Counting Adventure*

Teacher Voice

John used *Next Please* when constructing a DLTA for his kindergarten students. He decided to use this book because it would provide students with opportunities to make predictions. He also realized that students could relate to the story because most if not all had been to a doctor's office and had had to wait in the waiting room. After setting the purpose for listening, he asked students to share their experiences with going to a doctor's office. After providing time for students to share their thoughts, he showed students the book and asked them to make some predictions using their previous discussion and by looking at the cover of the book. He then began reading the story and stopped after the ladybug came out of the office and asked, "Which character is going to be next? How do you know?" He turned the page and used the picture to confirm students' predictions. He continued reading until the last character came out and asked, "What do you think will happen now?" After students shared their ideas, he turned the page to reveal the blank pages at the end of the book and asked students, "Why do you think these pages are blank?"

Students checked their predictions throughout the reading of the story. To bring the DLTA to a close, John asked students to summarize what happened. He then reminded students that making predictions is important because it keeps listeners involved in the story. It also helps them think about what the author is sharing with them.

Extensions/Tips/Connections

1. To help students become comfortable with making predictions in all subject areas, provide time for students to preread questions and make some predictions about possible answers. After listening, students can return to the questions and talk about which, if any, have been answered.

2. Sneak Preview (DeHaven 1989) provides a slight variation of the DLTA. After reading or telling part of a story such as *George Upside Down* or describing an event, stop and ask children to think about what they have heard and make illustrations showing their predictions of the next event. Students then share their pictures and tell why they think the events might happen. Continue reading and have students confirm or adjust their predictions.

3. ELVES (excite, listen, visualize, extend, savor; Levesque 1989) is another way to use listening to help students learn to make predictions. It begins with a discussion that connects the listeners' personal experiences to the story. The reader then asks listeners to make predictions about the story using cues from the previous discussion and by looking at the book cover and title (i.e., the reader gets listeners *excited* about the story). Next, listeners *listen* to the story and simultaneously think about their predictions. The reader also invites children to *visualize* characters and events while listening to the story. These are used when discussing the story. Fourth, the reader *extends* the story by asking questions that encourage deeper thinking about the story. Finally, listeners *savor* and reflect on the story and connect it with their lives. For example, the reader might ask, "Would you like to trade places with one of the characters?"

STRUCTURED LISTENING ACTIVITY (SLA)
Questioning

GRADE LEVEL: 2-6

Description

The Structured Listening Activity (Choate and Rakes 1987) enables teachers to use specific procedures to teach listening. Each of the six steps echoes recommendations for teaching reading comprehension. For example, recognizing the importance of background knowledge, the second step is to prepare the listeners by relating the content to students' experiences and to discuss any necessary terminology that will facilitate comprehension. The fifth step focuses on questioning, an important element of reading comprehension. The same is true for listening comprehension. The questioning focuses on the types of questions asked and students' abilities to self-monitor. Learners are expected to explain answers to questions they have asked of the text. Being able to answer these questions shows that the learner comprehended. Let's remember that the purpose of listening is comprehension.

Teaching Suggestions

(These are based on Choate and Rakes [1987].)

1. Select the reading material.

2. Build concepts. This can be accomplished by introducing the reading material to students and relating it to something in their lives. Also, tap pertinent background experiences. Present any necessary vocabulary.

3. Set the purpose for listening. Provide students with important points you want them to listen for.

4. Read the text aloud and provide opportunities for students to make predictions by asking questions such as, "What do you think will happen next? Why do you think so? What tells or shows you that?"

5. Use questions to guide and assess listening comprehension before, during, and after the listening experience. Remember to use both literal questions as well as interpretive or critical questions. Provide time for students to explain their answers. Asking questions during the listening experience provides students with additional thinking. Asking questions after the listening experience is one way to check students' self-monitoring as well as start a discussion.

6. Have students summarize the text. You might want to assist by having them think of how the who, what, why, and when relate to the text.

Suggested Titles

Rick Chrustrowski, *Hop Frog*

Kathleen Krull, *Harvesting Hope*

Ted Lewin, *Lost City: The Discovery of Machu Picchu*

Jerdine Nolen, *Pickle Museum*

Darcy Pattison, *The Journey of Oliver K. Woodman*

Jean Richards, *How the Elephant Got Its Trunk*

Tony Ross, *Centipede's 100 Shoes*

Teacher Voice

Josh wanted to provide his fourth-grade students with a structured listening activity to enhance their listening comprehension. He selected *Lost City: The Discovery of Machu Picchu* for the text because it would be an excellent way to have students focus on listening while learning more about world geography. He also thought that the book would captivate students' interests because it focuses on something mysterious. Further, the story involves the boy who led the explorer Hiram Bingham to the site of Machu Picchu. After inviting students to tell about some of their discoveries, he told students that the purpose for listening to today's text was to determine how Machu Picchu was discovered. He began reading aloud stopping at points to ask questions to further guide students' listening. Once he read the entire book, he asked students to talk about the book using questions such as "So how was Machu Picchu discovered? Why do you think the boy was so willing to take the explorer to the site? Would you have taken a stranger to the site? Why or why not?" Josh closed the lesson by having students summarize the text. He invited volunteers to share who, what, why, and when as a part of this class summarization.

Extensions/Tips/Connections

1. Swafford and Paulos (1993) offer an in-depth explanation that shows how they used the SLA in a science lesson. They also pose questions that teachers can use to plan lessons that integrate listening.

2. Inviting students to preview a book and prepare questions is a natural activity. *Harvesting Hope* is but one title that can be used. Questions can focus on the different aspects of Cesar Chavez's life.

3. *How the Elephant Got Its Trunk* is a perfect book to show students how questions are sometimes generated in the text and are used to tell the story.

SUM IT UP!
Summarizing

GRADE LEVEL: K-6

Description

The essence of listening is comprehension. As mentioned in Chapter 1, listening goes beyond simply hearing the sounds, as in discriminative listening. Listening is an active process through which the message is analyzed and interpreted. One way to assist this listening comprehension is to summarize what you have heard. Summarizing while listening is especially important because it helps the listener be aware of what she's being told. Throughout their school years, children need to listen to longer and longer passages and stories, and being able to summarize them *while* listening is important, because it helps children focus on important aspects of the story or lecture. Sum It Up is designed to start children on the right path when listening to and summarizing longer stories.

Teaching Suggestions

1. Select a children's literature selection to read aloud, focusing on a story that can be broken down into parts. Before you read the book to the children, find good stopping points where you can have students summarize chunks of the text.

2. Remind the students it is important to listen to the entire story, but sometimes you can break stories into parts. Tell them that you will be stopping frequently, so they need to be ready to summarize sections of the story.

3. To help model for the children, read to your first stopping point and then summarize what has happened for them. Then continue reading, asking the class to summarize chunks of the story along the way.

4. At the end of the book have the students put their different summary chunks together to summarize the entire story. Write all the sections on the board from start to finish.

5. Read the summaries as a group.

Suggested Titles

Julia Donaldson, *The Spiffiest Giant in Town*

Bob Graham, *Benny: An Adventure Story*

David McPhail, *Big Brown Bear's Up and Down Day*

Jean L. S. Patrick, *Cows, Cats, and Kids: A Veterinarian's Family at Work*

Janet Pedersen, *Millie in the Meadow*

Ken Stark, *Oh, Brother!*

Helen Stephens, *Blue Horse*

Teacher Voice

Janet saw that her second graders were ready to listen to longer books. She pulled the book *Big Brown Bear's Up and Down Day* off her shelf. She knew this book was divided into sections, a picture book with small "chapters." Janet told her students that they would be stopping at the end of each chapter to summarize it, so they needed to listen to what happened in each chapter. Janet noticed that while she read, her students were more attentive to the story than usual. When she stopped at the end of each chapter, as she promised, her students were eager to share what happened and summarize the story. Janet decided to take her idea one step further and at the end of the book asked the students to share their summaries in order. She wrote their sequenced summaries on a piece of chart paper so the students would be able to see how successful their listening was. Janet reminded her students that summarizing helps listeners understand stories or what they are listening to.

Extensions/Tips/Connections

1. Share with Me: After reading a book to the class, have students talk in pairs about the story they just heard. Have each pair create its own summary of the story. Then have the pair join another pair. Have these groups of four share their summaries and adapt their summaries to create a new common summary. Double the groups one more time, so you have groups of eight sharing and then creating common summaries.

2. First, Second, Third . . . : Sometimes students struggle with the order of things when they summarize a story. Before reading a book to children, have them divide into groups of four. Ask each group to decide which members will be responsible for summarizing the first, second, third, and fourth parts of the story. As you read, the students listen to the story and get ready to share their parts of the story. Have them share their parts of the story with their groups. After the groups have shared, read the story to the students again and stop to discuss whether or not their summaries flowed the same way as the story.

3. Newspaper Reporter: Invite the students to imagine that they are newspaper reporters. After listening to the story, they must come up with a headline that summarizes what happened in the story.

GET THE PICTURE
Visualization

GRADE LEVEL: K-6

Description

Visualization is a key aspect of comprehension, especially when listening. When listening to a book being read aloud, children are constantly asked to create a "movie in their mind" (Duke and Pearson 2002). Creating a visual of what is happening is a crucial beginning to comprehension while reading as well. Teachers can work with students to help them with visualization. Get the Picture is designed to help students allow their images to come to life as well as assist them in listening comprehension.

Teaching Suggestions

1. Choose a children's literature selection to read aloud that has illustrations that create strong visualization of the story.

2. Give students paper and crayons, markers, colored pencils, and so on. Tell the students they will be creating their own illustrations for the story.

3. Read one page to the students and allow them time to illustrate the page. Keep the book's illustrations hidden so as not to influence the class.

4. Continue reading and allowing time for illustrations. **Note:** This activity may take some time, so it's a good idea to stretch it out over a couple of periods.

5. Have each student share his or her illustrations with a partner.

6. Reread the book to the class and allow the children to see the pictures from the book.

Suggested Titles

Saxton Freymann, *Baby Food*

Linda Oatman High, *The Girl on the High-Diving Horse*

Kathleen Kranking, *The Ocean Is . . .*

Jonathan London, *Giving Thanks*

Helen Ward, *The Dragon Machine*

Teacher Voice

Third-grade teacher Sara became aware that her students were starting to read longer books. She knew visualization would be a key strategy that would help them comprehend the longer books. She decided to start visualization through listening. Sara selected *The Ocean Is . . .* and told her students they would be doing the illustrations for the book. As she got ready to read, she told the students to listen carefully to what she read and to draw and color whatever they saw in their minds, based upon what they heard. Reading only the first sentence from each page, Sara allowed the students to illustrate their own images. She did not show the students the pictures from the book, instead allowing them the chance to create their own. After they finished the book she had her students pair up and share their illustrations. There was much laughter and approval of classmates' drawings. Sara then brought the students back together and read the book to them again, this time showing the pictures to the children. During this reading the students shared questions and comments about the illustrations as compared with their illustrations. Sara reminded the students that visualization is an important part of comprehending, and listening is a good place to start visualizing. By creating pictures in their minds, they could begin to follow along with a story.

Extensions/Tips/Connections

1. Postcards from the Story: While reading a children's literature selection to the students, give them each a postcard-sized piece of white construction paper. Have them draw a scene from the book as the postcard's picture. On the other side of the postcard, have the students write a quick note to one of the characters in the story.

2. Draw with Me: Using a book like *The Dragon Machine*, read the first page to the class. Put the book down and ask the students what they see on that page. As they tell you, draw the picture on a piece

of chart paper. Include all the different possible details. Continue this process with every page in the book. When the book is complete, have the students help you put the pictures in the correct order. This activity helps children work with two different concepts: visualization and sequencing.

3. Do You See What I See? Using two picture books with different types of illustrations, such as *Baby Food* and *Giving Thanks*, read one book to the students. As you read, talk about the illustrations with the class. Ask students what they notice about the illustrations or what jumps out at them. Then read the other book to them. Have them compare the illustrations and talk about what they notice. Point out to the class that pictures can be different, but they always play an important role in the book. Discuss how what they see when they hear a book is important in understanding the story.

CHAPTER 4 TITLES

FILL IN THE GAPS

Lewis, Paul Owen. 2003. *The Jupiter Stone*. Berkeley, CA: Tricycle.

Singer, Marilyn. 2003. *Fireflies at Midnight*. New York: Atheneum.

Wood, Audrey. 2003. *Alphabet Mystery*. New York: Scholastic.

Yee, Wong Herbert. 2003. *Tracks in the Snow*. New York: Henry Holt.

DIRECTED LISTENING-THINKING ACTIVITY

Howard, Arthur. 2003. *Serious Trouble*. San Diego: Harcourt.

Ichikawa, Satomi. 2002. *My Pig Amarillo*. New York: Philomel.

Jandl, Ernst. 2002. *Next Please*. New York: Putnam.

McCarthy, Meghan. 2003. *George Upside Down*. New York: Viking.

Minchella, Nancy. 2003. *Mama Will Be Home Soon*. New York: Scholastic.

Noonan, Julia. 2003. *Mouse by Mouse: A Counting Adventure*. New York: Dutton.

STRUCTURED LISTENING ACTIVITY

Chrustrowski, Rick. 2003. *Hop Frog*. New York: Holt.

Krull, Kathleen. 2003. *Harvesting Hope*. San Diego: Harcourt.

Lewin, Ted. 2003. *Lost City: The Discovery of Machu Picchu*. New York: Philomel.

Nolen, Jerdine. 2003. *Pickle Museum*. San Diego: Harcourt.

Pattison, Darcy. 2003. *The Journey of Oliver K. Woodman*. San Diego: Harcourt.

Richards, Jean. 2003. *How the Elephant Got Its Trunk*. New York: Holt.

Ross, Tony. 2002. *Centipede's 100 Shoes*. New York: Holt.

SUM IT UP!

Donaldson, Julia. 2002. *The Spiffiest Giant in Town*. New York: Dial.

Graham, Bob. 2003. *Benny: An Adventure Story*. Cambridge, MA: Candlewick.

McPhail, David. 2003. *Big Brown Bear's Up and Down Day*. San Diego: Harcourt.

Patrick, Jean L. S. 2003. *Cows, Cats, and Kids: A Veterinarian's Family at Work*. Honesdale, PA: Boyds Mills.

Pedersen, Janet. 2003. *Millie in the Meadow*. Cambridge, MA: Candlewick.

Stark, Ken. 2003. *Oh, Brother!* New York: Putnam.

Stephens, Helen. 2001. *Blue Horse*. New York: Scholastic.

GET THE PICTURE

Freymann, Saxton. 2003. *Baby Food*. New York: Scholastic.

High, Linda Oatman. 2003. *The Girl on the High-Diving Horse*. New York: Philomel.

Kranking, Kathleen. 2003. *The Ocean Is . . .* . New York: Holt.

London, Jonathan. 2003. *Giving Thanks*. Cambridge, MA: Candlewick.

Ward, Helen. 2003. *The Dragon Machine*. New York: Dutton.

5

Critical
Listening

The child with whom I (Michael) was watching television brought me into focus. The conversation went something like this:

"Is that really true?"

"What?" I responded.

"That if you feed your dog that kind of dog food it will never get sick."

"What do you think?" I responded.

"I don't think so," she said. "There are a lot of things that can make your dog sick and you have to get them shots if you want them to stay well."

"I have to agree with you. Aren't you glad that you can listen critically so that you can think through what others are trying to get you to buy?"

"I sure am. They just want us to buy that dog food."

It never ceases to amaze me just how much of what we learn comes from television or radio. In fact, as Devine (1982) noted several years ago, we learn more through television, radio, and movies than we do in formal schooling. For instance, how many times have you heard someone say, "How did you know that?" only to be told, "I heard it on the radio"? Without a doubt, speakers are in a very powerful position to influence listeners. Therefore, listeners need to be able to critically examine a message before accepting it.

Learning how to comprehend a spoken message and how to evaluate it is what critical listening is all about. It goes beyond the other forms of listening presented to this point because it calls on the listener to analyze the message rather than accept it at face value. It's as though

SKILL	WHAT'S YOUR PERSPECTIVE?	LOADED WORDS	PROPAGANDA	FACT AND OPINION	COMPARE AND CONTRAST
Recognizing emotive language		•			
Recognizing bias	•		•	•	
Distinguishing between fact and opinion			•	•	
Recognizing a speaker's implications	•		•	•	
Evaluating sources	•	•	•	•	•
Detecting propaganda techniques	•		•	•	
Determining relevant and irrelevant information	•	•	•	•	•

5-1.

Effective Critical-Listening Teaching Strategies and the Skills They Develop

the listener scrutinizes everything that is being said, looking for faulty logic or statements that lack supporting evidence. In essence, the critical listener has to be convinced that the speaker is credible and that he can substantiate what he is offering.

Perhaps one of the most important parts of listening critically has to do with forming some criteria that can be used to evaluate the speaker. For example, Wolvin and Coakley (1979) note that critical listeners need to be taught how to distinguish between a speaker's implications and factual information. In a sense, this is much the same as being able to distinguish between fact and opinion. Take a sports reporter's comments, for instance. The reporter might say, "The score of the Avalanche game was 3–0. The Avalanche won" (fact). She may then say, "This victory proves that they are the best team in the league" (opinion). Knowing how to distinguish between the two is important because the listener can then decide whether or not the statement holds true for him and how to best act on the information.

While *evaluation* is a key word when thinking about critical listening, there are other skills that pertain to critical listening. Figure 5–1 shows these skills along with the specific teaching strategies that can be used to help students develop them.

WHAT'S YOUR PERSPECTIVE?

GRADE LEVEL: K-6

Description

As discussed throughout this book, listening is a complex, active process. Listening to discern a given perspective is one important aspect of listening. It helps the listener better understand a story or speaker. It also helps the listener make some decisions about the credibility of the speaker's perspective and determine if there is any bias. Listeners can discover perspective by listening for how the story is being told (i.e., voice). For example, are listeners hearing a lot of "I"s? If so, then the story is in first person and is biased in favor of the individual telling the story. If the story contains "he (or she) did this," then it is narrated in third person. Without a doubt, determining the perspective or bias requires the listener to listen critically, which is exactly what this teaching strategy facilitates.

Teaching Suggestions

1. Choose a children's literature selection that focuses on different perspectives or presents one person's biased view of a story.

2. Set the purpose for listening. Tell the students to listen for whose perspective is being told in the story and if there is bias in the story.

3. Once you've read the story, ask the students what perspectives they feel were represented in the story. Ask for examples to support their points.

4. Reread the story and tell the students to stop you when you come to parts that support their identified perspectives.

5. Invite students to think of other stories or books they know in which multiple perspectives are represented.

Suggested Titles

Cain Bluthenthal, *I'm Not Invited?*

Barbara Bottner, *The Scaredy Cats*

Jeff Brumbeau, *Miss Hunnicutt's Hat*

Eve Bunting, *Whales Passing*

Elaine Greenstein, *Ice-Cream Cones for Sale!*

Deborah Hopkinson, *Girl Wonder: A Baseball Story in Nine Innings*

Julius Lester, *Shining*

Laurence Pringle, *Whales! Strange and Wonderful*

Douglas Wood, *Old Turtle and the Broken Truth*

Teacher Voice

Fourth-grade teacher Marv wanted his students to listen more critically to the stories that he read to them. To assist in teaching this strategy, he selected a book that contains different people's version of a story: *Ice-Cream Cones for Sale!* Before he began reading, Marv told his students they would hear different versions of the same event. He asked the children to listen critically to the read-aloud so they could determine if there was bias in each character's telling of the story. After he finished reading the story, Marv's class had a lively discussion of it. The students came up with many different ideas for who may have first invented the ice-cream cone. Marv asked his students to support their ideas. To assist them, Marv read the story to the class again, stopping and allowing the students time to point out specific examples that supported their claims. Marv concluded the lesson by pointing out how important it is to listen critically to what is being told to you. By determining the perspective, you can better comprehend what is being said and not be taken in by a biased view or only one perspective, or at least be aware that biases are present in stories.

Extensions/Tips/Connections

1. Which One? Some books can present two different perspectives about the same topic or idea. *Whales! Strange and Wonderful* and *Whales Passing* are two books that both discuss whales and how people treat and admire whales. Working with both these books would allow children the opportunity to examine which perspective is being represented in each book and determine bias.

2. What Do You Think? *Miss Hunnicutt's Hat* is another book that allows children to look at a story through different perspectives.

Everyone looks at Miss Hunnicutt's hats differently. Children can discuss how different people in the story view her hats and if those perspectives change. Children can also explain how they would feel if they were Miss Hunnicutt or another character in the story.

3. What About Me? *I'm Not Invited?* provides yet another example for students to examine perspectives. In this book children can examine how the two main characters have different perspectives related to the same event. While discussing the different perspectives, children can also examine how feelings can come into play when people view the same event differently.

LOADED WORDS

GRADE LEVEL: 1-6

Description

We select and use words to communicate ideas with others. Some of the words we use are free from emotional overtones, whereas others are not. For example, when reporting on a student she had been tutoring, a graduate student of mine (Michael) commented, "He doesn't *even* know the alphabet!" How different this sentence would have been had she left out the word *even*! *Even*, as used in this context, carries emotional overtones that convey to the listener a message such as "Wow! I can't believe that the child doesn't know the alphabet!" Without *even*, the sentence would simply state a fact as supported by the results of an assessment. All emotionally loaded words (i.e., emotive words) would be omitted.

Sometimes the words people use focus on feelings. Words such as *useless*, *wonderful*, and *insightful* are a few examples of words that connect to feelings. Connections to feelings can be powerful, leading the listener to be swayed by the message regardless of how credible it is.

How important it is for listeners to understand that words can be used to influence their thinking! Students must learn to be critical listeners to detect this. Loaded Words is intended to help them develop this aspect of listening.

Teaching Suggestions

1. Select a book that has several examples of emotive language. You could also use newspaper articles or advertisements that contain emotive language.

2. Brainstorm with students words that are used to arouse their emotions. Examples include *mother*, *love*, *life*, and *peaceful*.

3. Set the purpose for listening to the story. In this case, students are to listen for words that trigger their feelings.

4. Read the story.

5. Ask for volunteers to share their words after you've read the story. As they share, write the words on a chart for all to see.

6. Discuss with students how the ability to identify words that are intended to evoke their feelings can be helpful in their everyday lives.

Suggested Titles

Ali Bahrampour, *Otto: The Story of a Mirror*

Carol Carrick, *The Polar Bears Are Hungry*

Deborah Chandra and Madeleine Comora, *George Washington's Teeth*

Joy Cowley, *Where Horses Run Free*

Barbara Shook Hazen, *Katie's Wish*

Mary Hoffman, *The Color of Home*

James Howe, *Horace and Morris Join the Chorus (But What About Dolores?)*

George Ella Lyon, *Mother to Tigers*

Clifton Taulbert, *Little Cliff and the Cold Place*

Jane Yolen, *Raising Yoder's Barn*

Teacher Voice

Several observations led Rob to discover that his fifth-grade students needed to learn about how words can be used to sway their thinking. He began by having students name different products they used in their everyday lives, such as shampoo and toothpaste. He then provided time for students to talk about why they used specific brands. After this discussion, Rob pointed out to students that many times advertisements are designed to appeal to listeners' emotions, thereby creating a perceived need to buy the advertised product. "Sometimes," he noted, "words that trigger your feelings are used in advertisements to make you feel a certain way about the product. These feelings then cause you to buy the product. Let's name some of these words."

After the brainstorming, Rob continued. "Authors of books do the same. They offer their ideas through their books and use words that trigger your emotions making you feel certain ways about the different characters or events. I am going to read *Where Horses Run Free*. The author uses some words to trigger your feelings about wild horses.

Listen for these words and we'll share these words when the story is finished." After reading the story, Rob asked volunteers to share some of the words they noticed. Volunteers offered words such as *free, open, useless,* and *crowded.* Rob asked students why these words triggered their emotions and provided time for students to share what they thought the author was trying to get them to believe. After discussing the book with them, Rob reminded his students that authors and advertisers use words that appeal to their audience's emotions in order to sell an idea or a product. Knowing how to critically listen for these words can help the audience make informed decisions about whether or not to accept the idea or product.

Extensions/Tips/Connections

1. Using a story such as *Mother to Tigers*, read it once as is and again without the words that arouse feelings. Ask volunteers to share the differences between the two versions. Which version had the most impact? Why?

2. Have students find examples of statements that are free from loaded words. Then have students change some of the words by replacing them with emotive words. For example, children could change the sentence "She walked into the house" to "She stormed into the house."

3. Invite students to listen to a taped recording of television advertisements and write down or state all of the loaded words. Have students compare and contrast the words they identify and talk about why different individuals find different words emotive. As an extension of this activity, students could also take out any loaded words used in an advertisement, listen to it again, and note the difference when emotive words are not used.

PROPAGANDA

GRADE LEVEL: 4-6

Description

Commercials are a large part of television, radio, and most recently, movies shown in theatres. Most are designed to convince the listener to buy the product being advertised and sometimes facts are altered a bit to help with the convincing. For instance, while it is true that chicken is a good source of protein, is eating fried chicken as healthy as some advertisers claim? The answer to the critical listener is a resounding "no!" According to Devine (1982), there are six specific ways that facts can be distorted (i.e., propaganda devices). The first is *glittering generality*. It involves the use of very general terms such as *American way* to make the generality attractive enough so that listeners will not question the speaker's main point. *Testimonial* is a second tactic. This is when the persuader (i.e., advertiser) connects a product with a famous personality. For example, a football celebrity eats at a fast-food chain and contends that if it's good for him, surely it has to be good for everyone. After all, look at the condition of the athlete! The implied message is that the food must be substantial enough to fortify the best of athletic bodies. *Name-calling* is a third technique. This is when the advertiser or persuader tries to point out the bad attributes of a given product or idea so that it will be immediately rejected. Some politicians use this technique when running for office. *Transfer* is a fourth technique. This is when the persuader tries to transfer the authority and prestige of some individual or object to another in the hope that the person or object will be accepted. For example, when a celebrity advertises a cosmetic, the listeners are supposed to believe that they, too, will look like this celebrity if they choose to buy the product. *Plain folks* is a fifth technique. This is when a speaker tries to look like and appeal to an "ordinary" audience. In an effort to persuade the listeners, the speaker might dress and talk just like the audience to gain a vote of confidence. *Card stacking* is a sixth technique. It involves giving only the positive points and suppressing the unfavorable ones.

As can be seen, being able to listen to and evaluate a message that contains one or more of these propaganda techniques is essential to our lives. Knowing about them puts us in control of what we are being led to believe and can save us a tremendous amount of money and/or heartache. Can that new mop do all they say it can do? Highly unlikely. Will that politician, if elected, fulfill all of those grand ideas to help the poor and the elderly? Again, not too promising. In essence, then, knowing how to evaluate a message that contains propaganda helps us make informed decisions.

Teaching Suggestions

(These are based on Devine [1982].)

1. Explain the six propaganda devices. Give both the definition and an example for each. You may want to use the chart shown in Figure 5–2.

2. Select a book or some advertisements to read to children.

3. Set the purpose for listening by telling students that they are to listen for any propaganda devices that are being used.

4. Read the selection.

5. Provide time for volunteers to share their discoveries. As they share their ideas, write them next to the appropriate propaganda technique on the board.

6. Remind students why knowing how to listen for the propaganda techniques is important in their lives both in and outside of school.

Suggested Titles

Larry Dane Brimmer, *The Official M&M's Book of the Millennium*

Megan Bryant and Monique Stephens, *Mott's Apples Away!*

Liz Conrad, *Mott's Sip and Slurp*

Max Ehrmann, *Desiderata: Words of Life*

Kevi, *Don't Talk to Strangers*

Madonna, *Mr. Peabody's Apples*

Jerry Pallotta, *Twizzlers Percentages Book*

PROPAGANDA DEVICE	DEFINITION	EXAMPLE
Glittering generality	Using general terms to make the generality attractive enough so that the speaker's main point will not be questioned	A person running for office states, "I am the best person for this job because I believe in the American dream."
Testimonial	Connecting a product with a famous personality	A noted sports figure is shown wearing a certain brand of clothing.
Name-calling	Pointing out the negative attributes so that the idea or product will be rejected	An advertiser points out why individuals should visit a given fast-food chain over another because the food at the latter is so unhealthy. Specific attributes are pointed out such as high fat content.
Transfer	Transferring the authority of some individual or product to another in the hope that it will be accepted	A noted celebrity is shown wearing a certain brand of cosmetics. The slogan reads, "Look how wonderful you can look when you use this brand of cosmetics!"
Plain folks	An attempt to sound like ordinary individuals in order to win them over	A candidate running for school board comments, "You should vote for me. I grew up in neighborhoods just like yours and I understand the issues."
Card stacking	Listing all of the positive points and leaving out any information that is not supportive	An advertisement reads, "Make sure you eat this breakfast cereal every day because it is fortified with extra vitamins and is low in calories as well as sodium."

Propaganda Devices: Definitions and Examples

Teacher Voice

In listening to her fifth graders talk about the different shampoos they used, Karen realized that her students had fallen prey to advertisers' claims. She viewed this as a perfect opportunity to teach students about the propaganda techniques that advertisers use to get the general public to buy their products. She began by having students brainstorm the types of shampoo they used and why they used them. She then used their examples as she explained the propaganda techniques shown in Figure 5–2. After reviewing these techniques, she told students that sometimes authors also use propaganda techniques when writing their stories. She noted, "Not only do advertisers use propaganda techniques. You will sometimes see that authors use one or more of these techniques when writing their stories to get you to buy in to their ideas." She then went on to explain that she would read *Desiderata: Words for Life* and that students were to listen to identify examples of propaganda techniques the author used. After reading the book, Karen invited volunteers to share their discoveries and to provide reasons for their answers. She closed the lesson by stating, "Knowing how someone is trying to influence you is important. If you know what to listen for, you can evaluate the message to determine how much of it you should believe. In the end, this can save you from buying unnecessary products. It can also keep you from overpaying for products that are no better than a less expensive brand."

Extensions/Tips/Connections

1. Invite students to construct a chart listing all of the propaganda techniques on the left-hand side of the chart and examples on the right-hand side. Then have them listen for advertisements that use the various techniques, making note of them on their charts.

2. To sell one of their favorite books, invite students to each construct an advertisement using one of the propaganda techniques. After sharing the advertisements, provide time for classmates to talk about which technique was used in each and why they think that technique was used.

3. Provide time for students to talk about when using the propaganda devices might be acceptable. Start the discussion by asking, "When, if ever, is it okay to use a propaganda device?"

FACT AND OPINION

GRADE LEVEL: 2-6

Description

Many times throughout our lives we need to determine the difference between fact and opinion. Talk radio is a wonderful illustration of this. I (Matthew) was recently listening to a sports talk show, and two callers in a row called in to talk about the big game that had just occurred. Both callers talked about how the winning team deserved to win because the player and coach from the losing team had said something derogatory before the game. The host asked for the exact words that the coach and the player from the losing team had said and the callers hemmed and hawed. The host reminded all of the listeners that they needed to present *facts* only; they could not make things up. For children, listening provides an opportunity to distinguish between facts and opinions. Being able to determine what is fact and what is opinion helps children comprehend and leads them on the road to critical listening. When listening to a story, for example, they can listen to determine if a given story character is sharing a fact or an opinion. Fact and Opinion teaches children to listen for what is fact and what is opinion and understand how the two types of statements can impact the message they receive while listening critically.

Teaching Suggestions

1. Choose a children's literature selection that contains a character presenting both fact and opinion.

2. Before starting the book, take some time to explain facts and opinions. If the students haven't learned about them, this would be the time to present a short lesson about the two.

3. Before reading the book to the children, tell them to be listening for either fact or opinion. Remind them they will have to listen carefully in order to find the two. Then read the story.

4. After reading the book to the children, ask them what they heard that was fact and what was opinion. Make a list of their ideas on the board in two separate columns, Fact and Opinion.

5. Reread the story and stop where their ideas match up with the story. Reexamine whether their ideas were indeed fact or opinion.

6. Remind students that they need to be aware that speakers use both fact and opinion and they need to be able to detect the difference.

Suggested Titles

Shana Corey, *Players in Pigtails*

Nancy Cote, *It Feels Like Snow*

Laurence Pringle, *Come to the Ocean's Edge*

Shelley Tanaka, *New Dinos*

Mark Teague, *Dear Mrs. LaRue: Letters from Obedience School*

Teacher Voice

Rose saw that her fourth graders were starting to believe everything that they were hearing. She decided they needed to be able to distinguish the difference between fact and opinion. She selected the book *It Feels Like Snow*. She told the students that the woman in the story could predict the weather. She then set the purpose for reading, having the students listen for either fact or opinion statements. After they finished reading the book, Rose had a discussion with her class. They made two lists on the board for fact and opinion statements. After they finished the lists, she reread the book to her students and they revisited the lists to determine if all the ideas were in the right column. Rose reminded her class that being a critical listener and identifying fact or opinion statements can help a person not be swayed by someone's opinion.

Extensions/Tips/Connections

1. Children should also be aware that fact and opinion statements can sway what a person believes. Sometimes this can cause hurt feelings. *Players in Pigtails* can be used to help students see how opinion statements can influence people and affect their beliefs and feelings.

2. Television programs and commercials present myriad opportunities for examining fact and opinion. Teachers can bring in tapes of different programs and commercials. Children can listen for specific examples of fact and opinion as well as talk about why they are being used.

3. After exposing the class to several opinion statements, have the students change them into facts. Students will become aware of words that are used to create opinions and will be ready when they hear those words in the future. The reverse can be done for this activity as well, turning facts into opinions.

COMPARE AND CONTRAST

GRADE LEVEL: K-6

Description

Being able to compare and contrast ideas and stories is another aspect of critical listening. In order to distinguish between two different ideas or stories, children must be able to discuss what makes the two things different. Being able to apply this skill combines both critical listening and critical thinking. Through comparing and contrasting, we're better able to make the best decision possible after weighing all of the ideas about given products or stories. Similar to propaganda, mentioned earlier in this chapter, we all need to be able to compare items or ideas, whether they are embedded in stories or in advertisements used to sell products. Being able to describe differences and similarities between the ideas presented in stories or advertised products, we become critical listeners, readers, and consumers. That is, we are more aware and not reliant upon one particular idea, story, or product. The following activity is one way to help children compare and contrast while listening.

Teaching Suggestions

1. Choose a children's literature selection that focuses on two different ideas that children need to compare.

2. Before reading, remind students they need to be ready to compare and contrast the story they hear and that they will hear two different ideas in the book.

3. Read the story to the students.

4. After reading the story, discuss with the class what the two ideas were. Create a Venn diagram for the students to list the ideas and analyze the differences between them.

5. Reread the book and correct or add to any ideas on the board.

Suggested Titles

Lucille Colandro, *There Was a Cold Lady Who Swallowed Some Snow!*

Crescent Dragonwagon, *And Then It Rained . . .*

Verla Kay, *Homespun Sarah*

Daniel Kirk, *Jack and Jill*

Jon J. Muth, *Stone Soup*

Eileen Spinelli, *The Perfect Thanksgiving*

Teacher Voice

Third-grade teacher Herb decided to see if students were ready to compare and contrast ideas in stories. He selected *The Perfect Thanksgiving* to read to his class. He told the students they would be hearing a story about two different Thanksgiving dinners. He reminded them to listen for differences about the dinners. After reading the book to the class, Herb started a discussion comparing the two dinners. The class created a Venn diagram that listed the similarities and differences between the two dinners. Herb then read the book again so students could pick up on all the ideas listed in the Venn diagram. As the lesson closed, he reminded the children that being able to compare and contrast stories and ideas is a way for them to listen and think critically. He added that these skills would help their comprehension in both listening and reading. Herb also discussed how comparing and contrasting stories or products in their everyday lives would make them more critical listeners, readers, and consumers.

Extensions/Tips/Connections

1. A classic activity for comparing and contrasting is to use a well-known story and a unique version of it. *There Was a Cold Lady Who Swallowed Some Snow!* is a perfect example. Students can listen to the story and the original version, *There Was an Old Lady Who Swallowed a Fly*. After hearing both stories, students can compare and contrast the versions. **Note:** It is crucial that children already know the original version of the story or song, so there is no confusion.

2. Children can create their own versions of a story or song. Allow the students to use any story or children's song they know very well. Give them an opportunity to be creative, but have them keep their tales familiar to the original version.

3. *And Then It Rained . . . (and Then the Sun Came Out . . .)* is an example of a "flip" book. Children can see the difference between the

two types of weather on same day after they flip the book. The book looks at a day when it rains and then when the sun comes out. Children can listen carefully for how the weather influences the day for the different characters in the book.

CHAPTER 5 TITLES

WHAT'S YOUR PERSPECTIVE?

Bluthenthal, Cain. 2003. *I'm Not Invited?* New York: Atheneum.

Bottner, Barbara. 2003. *The Scaredy Cats.* New York: Simon and Schuster.

Brumbeau, Jeff. 2003. *Miss Hunnicutt's Hat.* New York: Orchard.

Bunting, Eve. 2003. *Whales Passing.* New York: Scholastic.

Greenstein, Elaine. 2003. *Ice-Cream Cones for Sale!* New York: Scholastic.

Hopkinson, Deborah. 2003. *Girl Wonder: A Baseball Story in Nine Innings.* New York: Atheneum.

Lester, Julius. 2003. *Shining.* San Diego: Harcourt.

Pringle, Laurence. 2003. *Whales! Strange and Wonderful.* Honesdale, PA: Boyds Mills.

Wood, Douglas. 2003. *Old Turtle and the Broken Truth.* New York: Scholastic.

Yolen, Jane. 2003. *Roanoke: The Lost Colony.* New York: Simon and Schuster.

LOADED WORDS

Bahrampour, Ali. 2003. *Otto: The Story of a Mirror.* New York: Farrar, Straus, and Giroux.

Carrick, Carol. 2002. *The Polar Bears Are Hungry.* New York: Clarion.

Chandra, Deborah, and Madeleine Comora. 2003. *George Washington's Teeth.* New York: Farrar, Straus, and Giroux.

Cowley, Joy. 2003. *Where Horses Run Free.* Honesdale, PA: Boyds Mills.

Hazen, Barbara Shook. 2002. *Katie's Wish.* New York: Dial.

Hoffman, Mary. 2002. *The Color of Home.* New York: Penguin.

Howe, James. 2002. *Horace and Morris Join the Chorus (But What About Dolores?).* New York: Simon and Schuster.

Lyon, George Ella. 2003. *Mother to Tigers.* New York: Atheneum.

Taulbert, Clifton. 2002. *Little Cliff and the Cold Place.* New York: Dial.

Yolen, Jane. 1998. *Raising Yoder's Barn.* New York: Little, Brown.

PROPAGANDA

Brimmer, Larry Dane. 1999. *The Official M&M's Book of the Millennium*. Watertown, MA: Charlesbridge.

Bryant, Megan, and Monique Stephens. 2003. *Mott's Apples Away!* New York: Penguin.

Conrad, Liz. 2002. *Mott's Sip and Slurp*. New York: Penguin.

Ehrmann, Max. 2003. *Desiderata: Words of Life*. New York: Scholastic.

Kevi. 2003. *Don't Talk to Strangers*. New York: Scholastic.

Madonna. 2003. *Mr. Peabody's Apples*. New York: Callaway.

Pallotta, Jerry. 2001. *Twizzlers Percentages Book*. New York: Scholastic.

FACT AND OPINION

Corey, Shana. 2003. *Players in Pigtails*. New York: Scholastic.

Cote, Nancy. 2003. *It Feels Like Snow*. Honesdale, PA: Boyds Mills.

Pringle, Laurence. 2003. *Come to the Ocean's Edge*. Honesdale, PA: Boyds Mills.

Tanaka, Shelley. 2002. *New Dinos*. New York: Atheneum.

Teague, Mark. 2002. *Dear Mrs. LaRue: Letters from Obedience School*. New York: Scholastic.

COMPARE/CONTRAST

Colandro, Lucille. 2003. *There Was a Cold Lady Who Swallowed Some Snow!* New York: Scholastic.

Dragonwagon, Crescent. 2003. *And Then It Rained . . . .* New York: Atheneum.

Kay, Verla. 2003. *Homespun Sarah*. New York: Putnam.

Kirk, Daniel. 2003. *Jack and Jill*. New York: Putnam.

Muth, Jon J. 2003. *Stone Soup*. New York: Scholastic.

Spinelli, Eileen. 2003. *The Perfect Thanksgiving*. New York: Holt.

6

Appreciative
Listening

My wife asked me (Matthew) about a song we were listening to in the car.

"What is he singing?" she asked. I told her what I thought the words were and she said it didn't make much sense. I thought about the words and the song all together and realized that it was a very difficult song to understand. Later we were listening to another music group, and I said, "I love the way the singers harmonize on this song." As we listened more closely, we heard how the voices matched and later how they sang completely different lyrics over each other. Little did my wife realize we were listening appreciatively.

Although we were discussing the different songs together, appreciative listening is quite individualistic, hence subjective. I heard and appreciated some parts, whereas my wife heard and appreciated others. As we listen, different aspects catch our attention and draw us in. However, there are many different aspects of appreciative listening we can focus on (e.g., words in songs, specific instruments, how everything blends together in a song). Wolvin and Coakley (1996) note that there are five different things we listen to appreciatively:

- oral style
- environmental sounds
- oral reading of literature
- radio, television, and film
- live theatre

Appreciative listening is the highest level of listening (DeHaven 1989), and you will find many examples of all the other chapters within this chapter.

In this chapter we examine different types of literature and how they can be used to teach appreciative listening. Poetry is one type that encourages appreciative listening. Many times reading poetry helps us see how a few words can create a big impact. Or using a book like *Joyful Noise: Poems for Two Voices* (Fleischman 1988) can show how two voices can create beautiful sounds as well. Humorous poetry can also elicit appreciative listening. Children enjoy language play and the humor it creates (Zbaracki 2003). Finally, this chapter will also examine how radio, television, film (which we will refer to as multimedia), and live theatre can be used to teach appreciative listening. Figure 6–1 shows the strategies suggested in this chapter and the skills they develop.

SKILL	HUMOR	POETRY	MUSIC	MULTIMEDIA	THEATRE
Recognizes physical attributes evoked		•	•		
Recognizes what he or she appreciates and why	•	•	•	•	•
Gains experience listening appreciatively in a variety of forms	•	•	•	•	•
Recognizes the pleasure listening appreciatively can bring	•	•	•	•	•
Aware of the different elements while listening appreciatively			•		
Recognizes feeling or mood that is evoked	•	•	•		
Recognizes the power of language	•	•			•
Appreciates the conciseness of language		•			
Appreciates how the words flow from the speaker	•	•		•	•
Appreciates oral interpretations	•				
Appreciates how music and other performing arts work together to evoke feeling		•	•	•	
Understands the power of imagination and how characters can evoke images			•	•	

6–1.

Effective Appreciative-Listening Teaching Strategies and the Skills They Develop

HUMOR

GRADE LEVEL: 2-6

Description

Laughter plays a large role in the lives of children. Enter any school and you will find children laughing, whether it is in the classroom or on the playground. Teachers can capitalize on children's laughter. Humor plays a big role in children's reading and does the same with their listening. In fact, listening is an excellent place to work with children and humor, because humor uses all the different types of listening we have discussed throughout the book. Appreciating the humor while listening invites children to listen critically. In order to understand a joke or the humor, all listeners must tend to every detail being shared. Some humor can be found in a different version of a well-known story, discovered through comparing and contrasting. Some humor, especially for younger children, can be found in the use of voice when reading a book. Humor can also be found in the use of language in books; because of this children must tend carefully to what is being told. One major advantage teachers have with listening and humor is that they can sense immediately if children are comprehending while they listen—laughter can be the key test of that. Being able to "find the funny" (Zbaracki 2003) is actually a skill that can be shared with children as they listen to different books and stories. This activity provides teachers with ideas to help children focus on the humor and appreciate how the humor might add to the story.

Teaching Suggestions

1. Choose a humorous children's literature selection.

2. Set the purpose for listening, and tell the students this is a humorous book, so they should listen for what they think is funny.

3. Remember, humor can be discovered quickly, so feel free to stop and discuss the elements of the story that make children laugh.

4. After reading the book, discuss with the students what impact the humor has upon the book. Give students the opportunity to discuss whether or not they feel they would have enjoyed the story without the humorous elements.

5. Reread the story all together. Hold a discussion at the conclusion about the book discussing the impact the humor has.

6. Tell children that it's okay to appreciate humor and that humor plays a big role in listening and reading.

Suggested Titles

Kathryn Madeline Allen, *This Little Piggy's Book of Manners*

Karin Ireland, *Don't Take Your Snake for a Stroll*

Laurie Keller, *Arnie the Doughnut*

Lisa Kopelke, *Excuse Me!*

Kate McMullan, *I Stink!*

Chris Raschka, *Arlene Sardine*

Teacher Voice

David noticed that his fourth graders enjoyed listening to humorous books. He found that these were the books his students went back to and reread numerous times. Eager to understand why, he decided to find out what his students appreciated about humorous literature. David selected the book *Arnie the Doughnut*. He told his students that they were going to listen to a funny book and that he wanted them to think about what made them laugh. Starting with the cover, David read the text, stopping occasionally to allow the students the opportunity to describe what they appreciated and why. The students happily provided explanations for the different attributes of the book they found humorous. David then reread the book and the children discussed what made the book so appealing to them. David reminded them that humor is not the only place to appreciate literature, or language, but it is a great place to start.

Extensions/Tips/Connections

1. The use of voice plays a big part with humor. Choose a book such as *Arlene Sardine* or *I Stink!* Read the book once to the children in a regular voice. Reread the book to them a second time using a different

voice (e.g., in *Arlene Sardine* use a New York accent; in *I Stink!* use a loud, gruff voice). Discuss with the students which version they appreciated more and why.

2. Select two different books. Choose one that is humorous and one that is not. Compare the two books and what makes them different. As a group, discuss ways the books could be changed to add or remove humor.

3. Much of humor can be visualized. Throughout this book we have discussed different ways listening promotes visualization. Select a book such as *Don't Take Your Snake for a Stroll*. Read the book to the children. As you read, allow children to draw or discuss with partners what they visualize the picture to be before you show it to them. Allow children to discuss with one another how they created their visualizations.

POETRY

GRADE LEVEL: K-6

Description

Appreciative listening can come in a variety of forms. Poetry provides one way to teach appreciation. Many times poetry can have a negative connotation with both teachers and students. One main reason for this is because more often than not, poetry is analyzed rather than enjoyed. As Janeczko (2003) states, "Reading a poem should not be like performing an autopsy, looking at a dead object and figuring out what killed it. Or worse, trying to figure out what it might have been like when it was alive. Good poems *are* alive . . ." (p. 10). Appreciating poetry is one way to make poetry come alive in your classroom. The flow of language, the rhythm of the words, the limited amount of words—all of these are ways we can *all* listen appreciatively.

Teaching Suggestions

1. Choose a collection of poems for children.

2. Set the purpose for listening. Tell the children you will be reading a book of poetry to them, and they should listen for something they like in the different poems. Also tell the students to create a visual in their minds of what each poem makes them think of. **Note:** Because the book will be made up of different poems, it will be much easier to stop and invite a discussion about the language or the images that children formed than when stopping during a storybook.

3. After you have read a few poems, allow students time to draw and share their images.

4. Next, you can put the pictures they drew up on a bulletin board with the poem or poems in the middle.

5. Alternatively, you could show the pictures to the children and remind them that everyone appreciates poetry differently and that the different images are what make poetry so much fun.

Suggested Titles

Rebecca Kai Dotlich, *In the Spin of Things: Poetry of Motion*

Paul Fleischman, *Joyful Noise: Poems for Two Voices*

Douglas Florian, *Bow Wow Meow Meow*

Sara Holbrook, *By Definition: Poems of Feelings*

Lee Bennett Hopkins, *Alphathoughts*

Tony Johnston, *The Ancestors Are Singing*

Ramona Maher, *Alice Yazzie's Year*

Takayo Noda, *Dear World*

Carol Diggory Shields, *Almost Late to School and More School Poems*

Charles R. Smith, *Hoop Queens*

William Jay Smith, *Up the Hill and Down: Poems for the Very Young*

Allan Wolf, *The Blood-Hungry Spleen*

Janet S. Wong, *Minn and Jake*

Jane Yolen, *Least Things: Poems About Small Natures*

Teacher Voice

Chris noticed that his third graders were having a hard time getting into all the different poetry books he had in the classroom. Being a big fan of poetry, he decided to take on a new approach. Chris selected *Dear World* to read to his class. Before reading, he told his students to listen for the use of language and see if the words helped make pictures in their minds. He read a few poems to the children and then stopped and asked for what pictures they made and how they felt about the flow of the words in the book. The students were eager to share their different ideas about the language and the pictures they saw. Chris decided to extend the lesson and work with their excitement. He told the students to now draw what they saw as he read the poems from the book. He stopped after one poem, "Dear Snow," and gave them time to finish their drawings. After they had all finished drawing, he put the drawings on a bulletin board, and in the center, he put a copy of the poem. Chris reminded his class that part of appreciating poetry is the fact that everyone has a different image when he or she listens to the words. He told the students how much he looked forward to sharing more poetry with them and helping them find poetry in their everyday lives.

Extensions/Tips/Connections

1. One of the best things to do with poetry and appreciative listening is to read a poem to your students every day. I (Matthew) once suggested this to one of my graduate classes in children's literature. I received an e-mail from the student about three months after the class. She told me that she had been reading a poem to her class every day as was suggested, but that things had become busy and she had run out of time. This occurred for about a week, she wrote, and then one of her students put up his hand and asked why she had stopped. The rest of the children joined in and admitted they were very disappointed that she was no longer reading aloud poetry to them. The class had learned to appreciate its poetry time.

2. Because poetry uses very few words, you can have discussions about the different words poets use. For example, read a poem from Jane Yolen's *Least Things: Poems About Small Natures*. The poems are quite short but create easy images for children. The students can discuss which words helped them create those images and how powerful those few words can be.

3. Some poems can get students involved in the reading. David McCord's "Pickety Fence" encourages students to make the sound of a stick whacking against a picket fence. Having the students make the sound all the way through the poem adds to the rhythm of the words. Involving students in this way helps lead to the discussion of how rhythm plays a big role in the poem.

MUSIC

GRADE LEVEL: K-6

Description

Music plays a big part in everyone's life, especially children's. Children enjoy singing different songs that they hear and will sing the same songs again and again. The use of music is a wonderful tool to help children become familiar with the specific ways language is used. Music and songs can also be used to tell different stories. As discussed at the beginning of this chapter, there are many different features of music that children can appreciate. DeHaven's (1989) belief that appreciative listening is the highest form of listening is quite apparent with music. There are many different attributes of music that children can identify and describe their appreciation for. This section provides different ideas to help children focus their appreciative listening.

Teaching Suggestions

1. Choose a selection from children's literature that is combined with a song and preferably comes with a tape of the song for children to listen to.

2. Tell the students you have a song you'd like them to listen to and that it accompanies a book.

3. Play the tape, and turn the pages along with the song.

4. At the end of the song, invite the students to discuss what they heard while listening. Provide time for listeners to share what they heard. Write their responses on the board or chart paper.

5. Before replaying the tape, remind the students to listen for the different attributes they discussed earlier.

6. After listening a second time, provide time for discussion of what changed as they listened a second time. Discuss what different aspects they appreciated more and why.

Suggested Titles

Katharine Lee Bates, *America the Beautiful*

Mary-Chapin Carpenter, *Halley Came to Jackson*

Ella Fitzgerald, *A-Tisket A-Tasket*

Steve Goodman, *The Train They Call the City of New Orleans*

Keith Graves, *Three Nasty Gnarlies*

Will Hillenbrand, *Here We Go Round the Mulberry Bush*

Mary Ann Hoberman and Nadine Bernard Westcott, *The Lady with the Alligator Purse*

Mary Ann Hoberman and Nadine Bernard Westcott, *Mary Had a Little Lamb*

Mary Ann Hoberman and Nadine Bernard Westcott, *Skip to My Lou*

Stacy Innerst, *M Is for Music*

Melanie Davis Jones, *Pigs Rock!*

Betsy Lewin, *Cat Count*

Megan McDonald, *Baya, Baya, Lulla-by-A*

Metropolitan Museum of Art, *A Treasury of Children's Songs*

Lloyd Moss, *Music Is*

Fran Swift, *Old Blue Buggy*

Teacher Voice

Second-grade teacher Paul listened to his students come into school every day singing different songs from movies and the radio. He decided to see what they appreciated about music. Paul chose the book and tape *Halley Came to Jackson*. He told his students that they would be listening to a song that was also a book. He asked the students to listen to the song and be ready to describe what they heard and enjoyed about the song. After playing the tape and showing the students the corresponding pictures, he closed the book and asked the students what they thought. The students happily shared what they enjoyed about the song and the book. Paul listed their ideas on the board. He then told his students they would listen to the tape again, but this time he encouraged them to listen for something they saw on the list. After listening to the song a second time, Paul asked the students to share any new ideas they had. Another lively discussion occurred about the new aspects of the music that they appreciated. Paul reminded the students that whenever they listened to music, stories, or poetry, they could appreciate more than one aspect of it.

Extensions/Tips/Connections

1. Students can create their own versions of a made-up song found in a book. Using a book like *Three Nasty Gnarlies*, ask groups of students to create their own "tune" for the song. When the song comes up again in the text, allow each group to share its version of the song. While the words will be the same, the music will change, providing evidence that appreciative listening is subjective.

2. Some books have a natural flow to the words that lend themselves to song. In a sense, the reader is "catching the beat." Select a book that has this natural feature, such as *Cat Count*. Read the book to the students and allow them the opportunity to catch the beat. After they have the beat, reread the book, allowing them to read or sing along.

3. Classical music has plenty of different attributes to appreciate. Select many different classical music pieces, some from movies and some other selections children may not know. Play the music for the students and hold a discussion like the one described in the Teacher Voice section. This provides an opportunity for the children to hear multiple aspects of the same piece of music.

MULTIMEDIA

GRADE LEVEL: 1-6

Description

While humor, poetry, and music play a big role in appreciative listening, multimedia (i.e., film, radio, and television) provides numerous aspects to focus on as well. We have already discussed how talk radio influences listening; combine that idea with sound effects, and you have the old-time radio shows and old-time broadcasts of sporting events. Times have changed, and now when we listen to the radio, we might hear the actual sounds at a sporting event, such as the crowd cheering and the crack of the ball meeting the bat. There are many aspects to focus on when listening appreciatively. Even television and film provide different aspects to focus on. Is there a reason a character talks faster and faster? Why did his voice go soft? While we listen for the message the character might be telling us, there are also other features to focus on. This section provides examples of how film, radio, and television can be used to teach appreciative listening. We will focus on live theatre in the next section.

Teaching Suggestions

1. Choose an unfamiliar form of multimedia to listen to, for example, an old-time radio broadcast.

2. Tell the students they are going to hear a story told on the radio. Ask them to listen and be ready to discuss what they heard while listening to the story.

3. Play about half of the story for the students, then stop and have the students discuss what they heard. Help the students go beyond listening for comprehension. Encourage them to discuss what they heard as they listened to this "new" type of storytelling.

4. List the features they describe on the board or chart paper.

5. Tell the students when they listen to the second half of the story, they should focus on features they didn't notice during the first half, like those listed on the board.

6. After the conclusion of the story, invite the students to discuss what aspects they appreciated in this new format of storytelling.

Teacher Voice

Lilly is a third-grade teacher who wanted her students to appreciate listening to different forms of multimedia. She brought in a tape of an old radio show, *The Lone Ranger*. She told her students they would be listening to an old story from the radio. She asked them to listen and be ready to discuss features they enjoyed from the story. Lilly played the first half of the show for her class. Then she stopped the tape and asked her students to discuss what they thought of the story so far. She listed their ideas on the board and made sure they discussed specific attributes of what they heard as they listened to the story. Before restarting the tape, Lilly told her class to try to focus on new features, from the list, for example, while they listened to the second half of the story. After the story was over, Lilly again led a discussion with the class about this new format of storytelling. The discussion covered many of the same features from the first list, as well as new features. She reminded her students that appreciative listening involves listening to multiple aspects found within the same piece, whether it's a story, book, film, or television show. Lilly also told them that they could listen appreciatively in their everyday lives.

Extensions/Tips/Connections

1. Multimedia today features two forms that children are *very* familiar with: television and film. Show some short clips from both television and film and ask your children to compare and contrast similarities and differences in what they appreciate about the two forms.

2. Music and film are also very closely tied together. Select a clip from a movie that contains music that is an integral part of the scene. Allow the class time to discuss how the music influences that scene and how different music would change the same scene.

3. For a project, have the students create an audiotape of different forms of multimedia that create the same feeling or tone. For example, the students could put together a clip of radio shows, television shows, and movies that all lead to a dramatic scene or that all lead to a very sad moment. Provide time for them to share their clips and have the class identify what mood is being evoked.

THEATRE

GRADE LEVEL: 1-6

Description

One form of multimedia that stands alone is theatre. The stage provides many examples of different ways children can listen appreciatively. Whether it be a play, a musical, or an opera, each theatre production provides different opportunities to listen appreciatively. While Michael may love going to the opera, Matthew might enjoy the opera but prefer going to a musical such as *Joseph and the Amazing Technicolor Dreamcoat*. Part of learning to listen appreciatively is to have many opportunities to do so (Wolvin and Coakley 1996). Exposure to each of these forms of theatre provides us the opportunities to make connections and identify specifically what we like or dislike. While all are on the stage, there are similarities and differences that are worth examining. This section provides examples of how to work with students and the idea of theatre.

Teaching Suggestions

1. Choose a children's play that contains numerous parts so that all children can have a role.

2. Pass out the play and allow children to read through it once.

3. Select people for each role.

4. Before the first read of the play, tell the children to listen to how the whole play fits together and how each character might influence the play.

5. Read through the entire play in character.

6. At the end of the play, discuss different features that would influence the play. (Key features to point out would be reading with expression and how loud the actors' voices are).

7. Discuss how these features can be used to influence the appreciation an audience might have for the play.

8. Provide time to put on the play, and videotape a dress rehearsal so children can see and hear how their performance influences the play before they perform it for an audience.

Suggested Titles

Sue Alexander, *Small Plays for Special Days*

Coleman Jennings, *Eight Plays for Children: The New Generation Project*

Coleman Jennings, *Theatre for Young Audiences: Twenty Great Plays for Children*

Justin Martin, *Twelve Fabulously Funny Fairy Tale Plays*

Margaret McDonald, *The Skit Book: 101 Skits from Kids*

Teacher Voice

Roger decided that his fifth-grade students had experienced many different forms of appreciative listening. He felt it was time to put them to the test and see how they appreciated theatre. He selected a play for them to perform. He made sure to select a play that had many parts so that each student would be included in the play. He passed out a copy of the play to each student. He told them to read through it alone first and to think about the parts they would like to perform. After the students had read through the play, the class chose roles. Before the first reading, Roger told the class to listen to each character and how all the characters influenced the play. After the first reading of the play, Roger led a discussion about some aspects that influence enjoyment of a play. Some ideas that came up were whether or not each actor captures the mood or personality of his or her character. They also discussed reading with expression and using a loud voice in order to be heard. Roger told his students they would perform for their school. After weeks of preparation, the class held a dress rehearsal. Roger videotaped the dress rehearsal. The children watched the tape to discuss elements they liked and those they felt could be improved so the school would better appreciate their performance. The class play was a school success and Roger reminded his class that sometimes in order to appreciate theatre, it is best to be a part of it. He also reminded them that there are different forms of theatre, and that while they probably appreciate some, there are others they may not enjoy; however, there are shared attributes to examine appreciatively.

Extensions/Tips/Connections

1. While it may not be easy to conduct a complete play, watching a videotape of a play and one of a musical would lend itself to a wonderful compare-and-contrast discussion. After viewing the two, the students could discuss which they appreciated more and why. The class could also change the musical to a play and add music to the play to create a musical.

2. A shorter activity that also teaches how voice and reading with expression influence appreciation is readers theatre. Short selections from children's literature can be used, or children can write their own passages.

3. A field trip to an actual play or a musical would be an excellent way to allow children an experience for appreciative listening. Local community plays as well as larger productions would give students an opportunity to add to their experiences and allow them to discuss the aspects they do or do not appreciate.

CHAPTER 6 TITLES

HUMOR

Allen, Kathryn Madeline. 2003. *This Little Piggy's Book of Manners.* New York: Holt.

Ireland, Karin. 2003. *Don't Take Your Snake for a Stroll.* San Diego: Harcourt.

Keller, Laurie. 2003. *Arnie the Doughnut.* New York: Henry Holt.

Kopelke, Lisa. 2003. *Excuse Me!* New York: Simon and Schuster.

McMullan, Kate. 2002. *I Stink!* New York: Joanne Cotler.

Raschka, Chris. 1998. *Arlene Sardine.* New York: Orchard.

POETRY

Dotlich, Rebecca Kai. 2003. *In the Spin of Things: Poetry of Motion.* Honesdale, PA: Boyds Mills.

Fleischman, Paul. 1988. *Joyful Noise: Poems for Two Voices.* New York: HarperCollins.

Florian, Douglas. 2003. *Bow Wow Meow Meow.* San Diego: Harcourt.

Holbrook, Sara. 2003. *By Definition: Poems of Feelings.* Honesdale, PA: Boyds Mills.

Hopkins, Lee Bennett. 2003. *Alphathoughts.* Honesdale, PA: Boyds Mills.

Johnston, Tony. 2003. *The Ancestors Are Singing.* New York: Farrar, Straus, and Giroux.

Maher, Ramona. 2003. *Alice Yazzie's Year.* Berkeley, CA: Tricycle.

Noda, Takayo. 2003. *Dear World.* New York: Dial.

Shields, Carol Diggory. 2003. *Almost Late to School and More School Poems.* New York: Dutton.

Smith, Charles R. 2003. *Hoop Queens.* Cambridge, MA: Candlewick.

Smith, William Jay. 2003. *Up the Hill and Down: Poems for the Very Young.* Honesdale, PA: Boyds Mills.

Wolf, Allan. 2003. *The Blood-Hungry Spleen.* Cambridge, MA: Candlewick.

Wong, Janet S. 2003. *Minn and Jake.* New York: Farrar, Straus, and Giroux.

Yolen, Jane. 2003. *Least Things: Poems About Small Natures*. Honesdale, PA: Boyds Mills.

MUSIC

Bates, Katharine Lee. 2003. *America the Beautiful*. New York: Putnam.

Carpenter, Mary-Chapin. 1998. *Halley Came to Jackson*. New York: HarperCollins.

Fitzgerald, Ella. 2003. *A-Tisket A-Tasket*. New York: Philomel.

Goodman, Steve. 2003. *The Train They Call the City of New Orleans*. New York: Putnam.

Graves, Keith. 2003. *Three Nasty Gnarlies*. New York: Scholastic.

Hillenbrand, Will. 2003. *Here We Go Round the Mulberry Bush*. San Diego: Harcourt.

Hoberman, Mary Ann, and Nadine Bernard Westcott. 2003. *The Lady with the Alligator Purse*. New York: Little, Brown.

————. 2003. *Mary Had a Little Lamb*. New York: Little, Brown.

————. 2003. *Skip to My Lou*. New York: Little, Brown.

Innerst, Stacy. 2003. *M Is for Music*. San Diego: Harcourt.

Jones, Melanie Davis. 2003. *Pigs Rock!* New York: Viking.

Lewin, Betsy. 2003. *Cat Count*. New York: Henry Holt.

McDonald, Megan. 2003. *Baya, Baya, Lulla-by-A*. New York: Atheneum.

Metropolitan Museum of Art. 2003. *A Treasury of Children's Songs*. New York: Holt.

Moss, Lloyd. 2003. *Music Is*. New York: Putnam.

Swift, Fran. 2003. *Old Blue Buggy*. New York: Dutton.

THEATRE

Alexander, Sue. 2003. *Small Plays for Special Days*. New York: Clarion.

Jennings, Coleman. 1999. *Eight Plays for Children: The New Generation Project*. Houston: University of Texas Press.

————. 1998. *Theatre for Young Audiences: Twenty Great Plays for Children*. New York: St. Martin's.

Martin, Justin. 2002. *Twelve Fabulously Funny Fairy Tale Plays*. New York: Scholastic.

MacDonald, Margaret. 1990. *The Skit Book: 101 Skits from Kids*. North Haven, CT: Linnet Books.

7

Assessing
Listening

In order to best help students develop as listeners, we not only need to teach them how but also determine if we have been effective. Assessing listening is an integral part of teaching listening. As Lundsteen noted years ago, "There is much about testing that is inseparable, fortunately, from instruction. Probably the most productive testing is that which is also instructional" (1979, p. 96). Consequently, every listening activity in this book has a built-in assessment. That is, for each lesson, the after-listening component calls on students to demonstrate that they have, indeed, listened to the speaker and gleaned pertinent information.

As important as this is, it is but one piece of the listening profile mosaic. There are other pieces that need to be in place to complete the picture. Our focus is on using informal assessment techniques, for like Devine (1982), we believe that they are more useful to classroom teachers and that they can be easy to construct relative to a specific purpose.

This chapter addresses four components of listening assessment: teacher self-assessment, student self-assessment, dimensions (i.e., types) of listening assessment, and classroom environment assessment. Figure 7–1 shows these components and how they work together to create a listening profile. Listening assessment is multidimensional.

Perhaps the best way to focus on the different components of listening assessment is to ask ourselves three important questions: What do I want to know? Why do I want to know? How can I best discover it? Figure 7–2 shows how to ask and answer these three questions. Pages 117-128 provide directions for their use as well as sample reproducible forms.

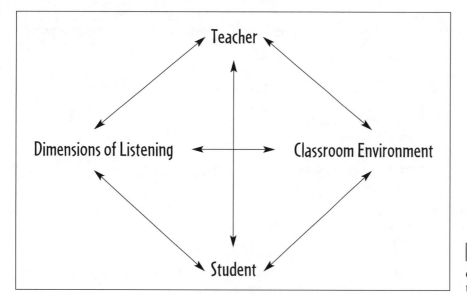

Teacher Self-Assessment

Given that adults listen with just 25 percent efficiency (Hunsaker 1990) and may be the worst listeners of all (see the introduction of this book), a good place to begin assessing is with ourselves. If we expect students to learn to be better listeners, then we ourselves must be better listeners. The good news is there are specific questions we can ask and answer of ourselves to better ensure that we are showing as much as telling students how to listen. Figure 7–3 shows some sample questions. Use the form as is or modifty it to fit your needs. You might also want to visit the International Listening Assocation's website (*www.listening.org*) to take the listening profile test.

An additional point that we need to make is that the active listening you model in your classroom should be based on some important beliefs about teaching and learning. According to Jalongo (1995), teachers need to believe that

- teacher talk is not always necessary for teaching and learning
- the focus is on learning how to think rather than gathering information
- questions need to encourage thinking
- children can construct viable questions
- all participants in the classroom need to listen to one another as well as the teacher
- listening and talking are ways to resolve problems and conflicts

Student Self-Assessment

Perhaps one of the best ways to engage students with learning and allow them to take ownership of their learning is to expect them to assess

WHAT I DO WANT TO KNOW?	WHY DO I WANT TO KNOW?	HOW CAN I BEST DISCOVER IT?
How well do I listen to my students?	Showing students how to listen is quite different from telling them how. I need to *model* what I expect from them. I need to be aware of how well I currently listen to them and if I need to improve. I am the one they will look to as they measure the importance of listening.	Teacher Self-Assessment Student Listening Interview
How do the students view their listening ability?	Change begins with awareness. Having children *attend* to different aspects of listening and evaluate themselves on each aspect will help them become better listeners. They will become more conscious about what they need to do to be better listeners.	Student Self-Assessment Student Listening Interview Self-Monitoring Questions
How well do students listen when expected to listen for a given purpose and for each type of listening?	There are specific reasons for listening. I need to know how well students can listen relative to a *specific purpose* to ensure that listening comprehension has occurred.	Classroom Listening Observation Form
Is the classroom environment designed to facilitate listening?	There are *environmental factors* that contribute to or detract from listening. These include room arrangement and room temperature. To ensure the best listening possible, I need to take a look at the classroom environment.	Classroom Environment Checklist

5-2.

The What, Why, and How of Listening Assessment

themselves. Not only does their self-assessment create a sense of ownership, it also helps them become aware of what they think about a given topic.

There are at least four ways to use student self-assessment as it pertains to listening. The first entails having students respond to questions about listening such as those shown on the interview guide in Figure 7–4. As a result of talking about listening, students better understand how they think about listening. The results of the interview can also help you clear up any misconceptions about listening that might be hindering students' understanding of it. For example, most often, students focus on physical characteristics such as sitting still and looking at the speaker when they are asked about effective listening. While these nonverbal behaviors contribute to listening, they certainly do not guarantee that listening is occurring. In fact, sometimes students focus so hard on attending to these external features that they forget to focus on comprehending the message, the essence of listening. If you discover that

Listen Hear!

Teacher Self-Assessment Form

Directions:

1. Make a copy of this form.
2. Read each question.
3. Think about the degree to which you perform each task.
4. Circle the appropriate numeral (1 = seldom; 5 = almost always).
5. Read the suggested activity for the areas that you want to improve.

Name _____ Date _____

QUESTION	RATING SCALE	SUGGESTED ACTIVITY
Do I listen to students without interrupting or allowing my attention to wander to other distractions in the room?	1　2　3　4　5	Time yourself when a student is talking to you. See how many minutes you can listen without letting your mind wander. Write down your time and work to expand it.
Do I demonstrate nonverbal behaviors such as giving eye contact, nodding my head, smiling, or giving some other facial expression to indicate that I have comprehended the message?	1　2　3　4　5	Look at students when they speak to you and make sure that you make the appropriate gestures to let them know you have heard them. Smiles, tears, laughter, disappointment—all are ways to show students that you listened to them.
Do I state directions clearly?	1　2　3　4　5	Keep your directions simple. Start with one- or two-step directions and increase them when you see that students can handle the simple directions. You can also have students repeat your directions after you give them. Doing so will let you take a second walk-through, listening for any additional information you need to share.
Do I explain the importance of listening to my students?	1　2　3　4　5	Talk with students about how you use listening in your life both in and out of school. Invite them to talk about ways they use listening, too. You might consider making and posting a list of these ideas.
Do I teach my students how to listen?	1　2　3　4　5	Use ideas mentioned in Chapters 2 through 6 to help students learn how to listen for specific purposes. Doing so will help them learn the different levels of listening and how they can use listening in their everyday lives.
Do I show students the importance of listening by integrating it with other subject matter throughout the day?	1　2　3　4　5	Effective listening instruction needs to be integrated with other course content. Consider using some of the lessons shown in this book as is or modify them to fit your content area.

7–3.

     (Continues)

QUESTION	RATING SCALE	SUGGESTED ACTIVITY
Do I set a listening purpose for students?	1 2 3 4 5	Write down what you want students to listen for. Make sure that you write this in a place where the entire class can see it. You might consider writing it on the board or an overhead transparency.
Do I prepare students for listening by making sure that they have the necessary background?	1 2 3 4 5	Use some sort of brainstorming activity before the lesson begins and write student comments on a chart or an overhead transparency. Revisit the chart after reading the story or making the presentation.
Do I assess students to ascertain their perceptions of listening?	1 2 3 4 5	Use the Student Listening Interview guide shown in Figure 7–4 to get a general idea of how students perceive listening. Use the results as you prepare listening lessons designed to heighten their understanding of listening.

7–3. ────────────

Student Listening Interview

Directions:

1. Make a copy of the Student Listening Interview form for each student.
2. Individually interview each student, making note of what he or she says on the form.
3. Use the results as you prepare meaningful lessons focused on listening.

Name _____ Date _____

1. When you are listening, what are you trying to do?

2. What helps you listen to others?

3. How can you tell when another person is listening to you?

4. What makes a person a good listener?

students view listening in this manner, you can design lessons to help them understand that listening is about comprehending. The majority of lessons shown in Chapters 2 through 6 are designed to help students do just that.

A second way to have students self-assess is to have them grade their performance on any or all of the after-listening experiences dovetailed into the listening lessons in Chapters 2 through 6. For example, as a result of the Give Me Five lesson, students should be able to state details from the story. They can prove they are able to do so by completing a listening guide similar to the one shown in Figure 3–3 (see page 40). Their performance is concrete evidence of the degree to which they were able to listen to a story or presentation and extract information related to the purpose for the listening experience.

A third way to have students self-assess is to provide them with a form similar to the one shown in Figure 7–5. A form like this can be used after a specific listening lesson or a lesson that has a listening component. Note that the first couple of questions focus on the nonverbal aspects of listening, whereas the remainder focus on listening comprehension.

Finally, students also can become more effective listeners by monitoring their understanding as they are listening. Being able to monitor is important because students have a better handle on when the listening comprehension is breaking down. They can then ask a question to clarify any misunderstandings (Tompkins 2002). As with other listening skills, however, students will need to be taught how to recognize that they don't understand the message. One way to help them with this is to provide them with some questions they can pose to themselves before, during, and after listening. Figure 7–6 shows some suggested questions. You might want to use them to construct a classroom poster or provide each student with his or her own copy. Then again, you might want to generate a list of possible questions with your students.

Assessing the Different Types of Listening

Chapters 2 through 6 have shown that there are different types of listening and presented some teaching strategies to help student learn how to listen at each level. As mentioned earlier, using the after-listening activities woven into the listening lessons shown in this book is perhaps the most authentic way to assess the degree to which students are able to listen for each type of listening (i.e., discriminative, precise, strategic, critical, and appreciative).

Another way to assess for the different types of listening is to develop an observation checklist and use it when observing students. Questions such as those shown in Figure 7–7 can be used to develop such

Student Self-Assessment Form

Name _____ Date _____

QUESTION	YES	SOMETIMES	NO
1. Did I look at the speaker?			
2. Did I keep still?			
3. Did I understand the story or the presentation?			
4. Can I talk to others about the story or presentation?			
5. Did I get the information I needed to get?			

What I did best when listening: _____

_____

One goal I have to be a better listener: _____

_____

7–5.

Suggested Self-Monitoring Questions

Before Listening

What is the purpose of listening?

Do I need to write something while I am listening?

Do I already know anything about what is going to be shared?

During Listening

Am I getting the information I need so that I can talk about this presentation?

Am I remembering what I need to remember, or should I write something down?

After Listening

Do I have any questions?

Can I state information related to the purpose for this listening experience?

7–6.

Discriminative Listening

1. Does the child demonstrate phonological awareness?
2. Can the child show how vocal expression can be used to affect listening?
3. Can the child provide examples of words that denote onomatopoeia?
4. How well can the child use nonverbal cues when listening?

Precise Listening

1. How well does the student associate words and meanings?
2. Can the child deduce the meaning of unknown words from context?
3. Does the child show understanding of grammatical structures?
4. Can the child form sensory impressions?

Strategic Listening

1. Does the child connect ideas and information?
2. Does the child connect prior knowledge with new information?
3. Can the child identify cause-and-effect relationships?
4. How well does the child summarize?

Critical Listening

1. Does the child recognize emotive language and its impact on listening?
2. Can the child recognize bias?
3. Does the child distinguish between fact and opinion?
4. Can the child detect propaganda techniques?

Appreciative Listening

1. Does the child listen to multiple features of stories, music, and multimedia?
2. Can the child discuss what gives him or her pleasure or enjoyment?
3. Does the child identify how he or she appreciates words in stories and musical lyrics?
4. Can the child discuss how the use of voice helps him or her better appreciate theatrical performances?

checklists for the different types of listening. Rather than trying to use all of the questions, consider choosing the question that best fits your purpose. Once selected, your observations can be recorded on a form such as the one shown in Figure 7–8.

7–7.

Suggested Observation Questions for Each Type of Listening

Classroom Environment

Any person familiar with elementary classrooms knows firsthand that there are several distractions that can potentially interfere with the best possible listening. Children and adults need to be able to tune out several noises in order to focus on the task at hand. If we truly want to help children learn to be the best possible listeners, we need to create

Assessing
Listening

Suggested Self-Monitoring Questions

Focal Question: _____

Context of Observation: _____ Date _____

NAME OF STUDENT	NOTES

7–8.

an environment that will facilitate the process. Yes, as minor as it might seem, the actual environment in which children are to listen is also important. If the temperature is too hot or too cold, for example, students will focus on this rather than on listening to the speaker. If chairs are arranged so that children cannot see the speaker, listening is not as likely. If a sense of community has not been established, children are not very likely to listen to one another. Clearly, paying attention to the environment is an important listening component.

One way to create the best possible listening environment is to think through the physical and psychological conditions that can potentially interfere with listening. According to Jalongo (1996), physical conditions include such things as fatigue, abuse, hunger, illness, bathroom needs, and room temperature. Psychological conditions include such things as attention span, ability to focus, language proficiency, interest in what is being shared, and self-esteem as a listener and learner. Here are eight suggestions for how you can use this information when establishing your classroom listening environment. Figure 7–9 shows how you can use these items in a checklist to ensure that you have considered each suggestion.

1. Make sure that children have health and hearing screenings.
2. Refer children for free breakfast or lunch programs as appropriate.
3. Arrange the room to provide for minimal distractions. For example, you might have a quite corner where children can go to when they need to be free from distractions in the rest of the classroom.
4. Arrange the furniture so that children can look at one another when they are speaking and listening.
5. Develop routines so that children know when they are to stop and listen to your directions. Some teachers use a song, whereas others use a chime.
6. Use visual reminders, such as a list of directions, for easy reference.
7. Expect children to listen to one another. One way to do so is to avoid repeating student answers or comments. If someone in the class cannot hear a classmate's comments, have the student repeat the answer. Likewise, if you feel that the student needs to speak more loudly, stand at different parts of the room and ask the student to repeat what was said so that you can hear him. The result? Students will begin to see that you value hearing them listen to one another as much as having them listen to you.
8. Provide a variety of listening experiences so that children learn to listen at different levels for different purposes. Again, Chapters 2 through 6 provide several suggestions to help you accomplish this.

Classroom Environment Checklist

Teacher's Name: _____ Date _____

QUESTION	YES	NO
1. Have I arranged for health and hearing screenings? **Comments:**		
2. Have I referred any children who need to be referred for free or reduced meals? **Comments:**		
3. Have I arranged the room so that there will be minimal distractions? **Comments:**		
4. Have I arranged the furniture so that children can look at one another when speaking? **Comments:**		
5. Have I developed routines so that children will know when they are to stop and listen to directions or when to switch activities? **Comments:**		
6. Do I have visual reminders posted where children can see them with ease? **Comments:**		
7. Have I stated to students the importance of listening to one another and modeled this by having students repeat their comments when others cannot hear them? **Comments:**		
8. Have I planned a variety of listening experiences for children to enhance their listening abilities at all levels (i.e., discriminative, precise, strategic, critical, and appreciative)? **Comments:**		

7–9.

Alexander, Martha. 2003. *I'll Never Share You, Blackboard Bear*. Cambridge, MA: Candlewick.

Alexander, Sue. 2003. *Small Plays for Special Days*. New York: Clarion.

Allen, Kathryn Madeline. 2003. *This Little Piggy's Book of Manners*. New York: Holt.

Andreae, Giles. 2002. *K Is for Kissing a Cool Kangaroo*. New York: Orchard.

Appelt, Kathi. 2003. *Piggies in a Polka*. San Diego: Harcourt.

Arnosky, Jim. 2003. *Armadillo's Orange*. New York: Putnam.

Ashman, Linda. 2003. *Rub-a-Dub-Dub*. San Diego: Harcourt.

Bahrampour, Ali. 2003. *Otto: The Story of a Mirror*. New York: Farrar, Straus, and Giroux.

Baker, Leslie. 2003. *The Animal ABC*. New York: Holt.

Bang, Molly. 2002. *Dawn*. New York: SeaStar.

Bates, Katharine Lee. 2003. *America the Beautiful*. New York: Putnam.

Bauer, Marion Dane. 2003. *Why Do Kittens Purr?* New York: Simon and Schuster.

Becker, Bonny. 2003. *An Ant's Day Off*. New York: Simon and Schuster.

Bluthenthal, Cain. 2003. *I'm Not Invited?* New York: Atheneum.

Bottner, Barbara. 2003. *The Scaredy Cats*. New York: Simon and Schuster.

Bright, Paul. 2003. *Quiet!* New York: Orchard.

Brimmer, Larry Dane. 1999. *The Official M&M's Book of the Millennium*. Watertown, MA: Charlesbridge.

Brisson, Pat. 2003. *Star Blanket*. Honesdale, PA: Boyds Mills.

Brown, Margaret Wise. 2003. *Sheep Don't Count Sheep*. New York: Simon and Schuster (McElderry).

Brug, Sandra Gilbert. 2003. *Soccer Beat*. New York: Simon and Schuster (McElderry).

Brumbeau, Jeff. 2003. *Miss Hunnicutt's Hat*. New York: Orchard.

Bryan, Ashley. 2003. *Beautiful Blackbird*. New York: Atheneum.

Bryant, Megan, and Monique Stephens. 2003. *Mott's Apples Away!* New York: Penguin.

Bunting, Eve. 2003. *Whales Passing*. New York: Scholastic.

Carle, Eric. 2001. *Where Are You Going? To See My Friend!* New York: Orchard.

Carpenter, Mary-Chapin. 1998. *Halley Came to Jackson*. New York: HarperCollins.

Carrick, Carol. 2002. *The Polar Bears Are Hungry*. New York: Clarion.

Cerullo, Mary M. 2003. *Sea Turtles: Ocean Nomads*. New York: Dutton.

Chandra, Deborah, and Madeleine Comora. 2003. *George Washington's Teeth*. New York: Farrar, Straus, and Giroux.

Cherry, Lynne. 2003. *How Groundhog's Garden Grew*. New York: Scholastic.

Chrustrowski, Rick. 2003. *Hop Frog*. New York: Holt.

Clark, Emma Chichester. 2003. *Follow the Leader!* New York: McElderry.

Cohen, Peter. 2002. *Boris's Glasses*. New York: Farrar, Straus, and Giroux.

Colandro, Lucille. 2003. *There Was a Cold Lady Who Swallowed Some Snow!* New York: Scholastic.

Conrad, Liz. 2002. *Mott's Sip and Slurp*. New York: Penguin.

Corey, Shana. 2003. *Players in Pigtails*. New York: Scholastic.

Cote, Nancy. 2003. *It Feels Like Snow*. Honesdale, PA: Boyds Mills.

Cowley, Joy. 2003. *Mrs. Wishy-Washy's Farm*. New York: Philomel.

———. 2003. *Where Horses Run Free*. Honesdale, PA: Boyds Mills.

Curlee, Lynn. 2003. *Capital*. New York: Atheneum.

Davies, Nicola. 2003. *Surprising Sharks*. Cambridge, MA: Candlewick.

Deacon, Alexis. 2003. *Beegu*. New York: Farrar, Straus, and Giroux.

Diakite, Baba Wague. 2003. *The Magic Gourd*. New York: Scholastic.

Dodds, Dayle Ann. 2003. *Where's Pup?* New York: Dial.

Donaldson, Julia. 2002. *The Spiffiest Giant in Town*. New York: Dial.

Dotlich, Rebecca Kai. 2003. *In the Spin of Things: Poetry of Motion*. Honesdale, PA: Boyds Mills.

Dragonwagon, Crescent. 2003. *And Then It Rained . . . .* New York: Atheneum.

Drummond, Allan. 2003. *The Flyers*. New York: Farrar, Straus, and Giroux.

Edwards, Pamela, and Henry Coles. 2001. *Slop Goes the Soup*. New York: Hyperion.

Ehrmann, Max. 2003. *Desiderata: Words of Life*. New York: Scholastic.

Elya, Susan Middleton. 2003. *Eight Animals Play Ball*. New York: Putnam.

———. 2003. *Oh No, Gotta Go!* New York: Putnam.

Farish, Terry. 2003. *The Cat Who Liked Potato Soup*. Cambridge, MA: Candlewick.

Farris, Cristine King. 2003. *My Brother Martin*. New York: Simon and Schuster.

Fisher, Valorie. 2003. *Ellsworth's Extraordinary Electric Ears*. New York: Atheneum.

Fitzgerald, Ella. 2003. *A-Tisket A-Tasket*. New York: Philomel.

Fleischman, Paul. 1988. *Joyful Noise: Poems for Two Voices*. New York: HarperCollins.

Fleming, Candace. 2003. *Boxes for Katje*. New York: Farrar, Straus, and Giroux.

Fleming, Denise. 2003. *Buster*. New York: Henry Holt.

Florczak, Robert. 2003. *Yikes!!!* New York: Scholastic.

Florian, Douglas. 2003. *Bow Wow Meow Meow*. San Diego: Harcourt.

Frazee, Marla. 2003. *Roller Coaster*. San Diego: Harcourt.

Freymann, Saxton. 2003. *Baby Food*. New York: Scholastic.

Garland, Michael. 2003. *Miss Smith's Incredible Storybook*. New York: Dutton.

George, Jean Craighead. 2002. *Frightful's Daughter*. New York: Dutton.

Glassman, Peter. 2003. *My Dad's Job*. New York: Simon and Schuster.

Goodman, Steve. 2003. *The Train They Call the City of New Orleans*. New York: Putnam.

Graham, Bob. 2003. *Benny: An Adventure Story*. Cambridge, MA: Candlewick.

Graves, Keith. 2003. *Three Nasty Gnarlies*. New York: Scholastic.

Greenstein, Elaine. 2003. *Ice-Cream Cones for Sale!* New York: Scholastic.

Harness, Cheryl. 2003. *Rabble Rousers: Twenty Women Who Made a Difference*. New York: Dutton.

Hartelius, Margaret A. 2003. *Knot Now! The Complete Friendship Bracelet Kit!* New York: Putnam.

Hazen, Barbara Shook. 2002. *Katie's Wish*. New York: Dial.

High, Linda Oatman. 2003. *The Girl on the High-Diving Horse*. New York: Philomel.

Hillenbrand, Will. 2003. *Here We Go Round the Mulberry Bush*. San Diego: Harcourt.

Hiscock, Bruce. 2003. *The Big Caribou Herd*. Honesdale, PA: Boyds Mills.

Hoberman, Mary Ann, and Nadine Bernard Westcott. 2003. *The Lady with the Alligator Purse*. New York: Little, Brown.

———. 2003. *Mary Had a Little Lamb*. New York: Little, Brown.

———. 2003. *Skip to My Lou*. New York: Little, Brown.

Hoffman, Mary. 2002. *The Color of Home*. New York: Penguin.

Holbrook, Sara. 2003. *By Definition: Poems of Feelings*. Honesdale, PA: Boyds Mills.

Hopkins, Lee Bennett. 2003. *Alphathoughts*. Honesdale, PA: Boyds Mills.

Hopkinson, Deborah. 2003. *Girl Wonder: A Baseball Story in Nine Innings*. New York: Atheneum.

Howard, Arthur. 2003. *Serious Trouble*. San Diego: Harcourt.

Howe, James. 2002. *Horace and Morris Join the Chorus (But What About Dolores?)*. New York: Simon and Schuster.

Ichikawa, Satomi. 2002. *My Pig Amarillo*. New York: Philomel.

Innerst, Stacy. 2003. *M Is for Music*. San Diego: Harcourt.

Ireland, Karin. 2003. *Don't Take Your Snake for a Stroll*. San Diego: Harcourt.

Isadora, Rachel. 2003. *Not Just Tutus*. New York: Putnam.

Jandl, Ernst. 2002. *Next Please*. New York: Putnam.

Jennings, Coleman. 1999. *Eight Plays for Children: The New Generation Project*. Houston: University of Texas Press.

———. 1998. *Theatre for Young Audiences: Twenty Great Plays for Children*. New York: St. Martin's.

Johnston, Tony. 2003. *The Ancestors Are Singing*. New York: Farrar, Straus, and Giroux.

———. 2003. *Go Track a Yak*. New York: Simon and Schuster.

Jones, Melanie Davis. 2003. *Pigs Rock!* New York: Viking.

Kay, Verla. 2003. *Homespun Sarah*. New York: Putnam.

Keller, Laurie. 2003. *Arnie the Doughnut*. New York: Henry Holt.

Kevi. 2003. *Don't Talk to Strangers*. New York: Scholastic.

Khan, Rukhsana. 2003. *Ruler of the Courtyard*. New York: Viking.

Kimmel, Elizabeth. 2003. *What Do You Dream?* Cambridge, MA: Candlewick.

King, Stephen Michael. 2000. *Emily Loves to Bounce*. New York: Philomel.

Kirk, Daniel. 2003. *Jack and Jill*. New York: Putnam.

Kolar, Bob. 2003. *Racer Dogs*. New York: Dutton.

Kopelke, Lisa. 2003. *Excuse Me!* New York: Simon and Schuster.

Kranking, Kathleen. 2003. *The Ocean Is . . . .* New York: Holt.

Krosoczka, Jarrett. 2003. *Bubble Bath Pirates!* New York: Viking.

Krull, Kathleen. 2003. *Harvesting Hope*. San Diego: Harcourt.

Kuklin, Susan. 2003. *All Aboard! A True Train Story*. New York: Orchard.

Lasky, Kathryn. 2003. *Before I Was Your Mother*. San Diego: Harcourt.

———. 2003. *The Man Who Made Time Travel*. New York: Farrar, Straus, and Giroux.

Leedy, Loreen, and Pat Street. 2003. *There's a Frog in My Throat!* New York: Holiday House.

Lester, Julius. 2003. *Shining*. San Diego: Harcourt.

Lewin, Betsy. 2003. *Cat Count*. New York: Henry Holt.

Lewin, Ted. 2003. *Lost City: The Discovery of Machu Picchu*. New York: Philomel.

Lewis, Paul Owen. 2003. *The Jupiter Stone*. Berkeley, CA: Tricycle.

London, Jonathan. 2003. *Giving Thanks*. Cambridge, MA: Candlewick.

———. 2003. *When the Fireflies Come*. New York: Dutton.

Long, Melinda. 2003. *How I Became a Pirate*. San Diego: Harcourt.

Lyon, George Ella. 2003. *Mother to Tigers*. New York: Atheneum.

MacDonald, Margaret. 1990. *The Skit Book: 101 Skits from Kids*. North Haven, CT: Linnet Books.

Madonna. 2003. *Mr. Peabody's Apples*. New York: Callaway.

Maher, Ramona. 2003. *Alice Yazzie's Year*. Berkeley, CA: Tricycle.

Martin, Justin. 2002. *Twelve Fabulously Funny Fairy Tale Plays*. New York: Scholastic.

Martin, Bill Jr. 2003. *Panda Bear, Panda Bear, What Do You See?* New York: Holt.

Mastro, Jim. 2003. *Antarctic Ice*. New York: Henry Holt.

McCarthy, Meghan. 2003. *George Upside Down*. New York: Viking.

McDonald, Megan. 2003. *Baya, Baya, Lulla-by-A*. New York: Atheneum.

McPhail, David. 2003. *Big Brown Bear's Up and Down Day*. San Diego: Harcourt.

McMullan, Kate. 2002. *I Stink!* New York: Joanne Cotler.

Meadows, Michelle. 2003. *The Way the Storm Stops*. New York: Holt.

Metropolitan Museum of Art. 2003. *A Treasury of Children's Songs*. New York: Holt.

Minchella, Nancy. 2003. *Mama Will Be Home Soon*. New York: Scholastic.

Mitton, Tony. 2002. *Dinosaurumpus!* New York: Orchard.

———. 2002. *Goodnight Me, Goodnight You*. New York: Little, Brown.

Moss, Lloyd. 2003. *Music Is*. New York: Putnam.

Munsch, Robert. 2003. *Lighthouse: A Story of Remembrance*. New York: Scholastic.

Muth, Jon J. 2003. *Stone Soup*. New York: Scholastic.

Myers, Walter Dean. 2003. *Blues Journey*. New York: Holiday House.

Newman, Leslea. 2003. *Pigs, Pigs, Pigs*. New York: Simon and Schuster.

Niven, Penelope. 2003. *Carl Sandburg: Adventures of a Poet*. San Diego: Harcourt.

Noda, Takayo. 2003. *Dear World*. New York: Dial.

Nolen, Jerdine. 2003. *Pickle Museum*. San Diego: Harcourt.

Noonan, Julia. 2003. *Mouse by Mouse: A Counting Adventure*. New York: Dutton.

O'Neill, Mary. 1966. *The Sound of Day, the Sound of Night*. New York: Farrar, Straus, and Giroux.

Pallotta, Jerry. 2001. *Twizzlers Percentages Book*. New York: Scholastic.

Patrick, Jean L. S. 2003. *Cows, Cats, and Kids: A Veterinarian's Family at Work*. Honesdale, PA: Boyds Mills.

Pattison, Darcy. 2003. *The Journey of Oliver K. Woodman*. San Diego: Harcourt.

Pedersen, Janet. 2003. *Millie in the Meadow*. Cambridge, MA: Candlewick.

Polacco, Patricia. 2003. *G Is for Goat*. New York: Philomel.

Pringle, Laurence. 2003. *Come to the Ocean's Edge*. Honesdale, PA: Boyds Mills.

———. 2003. *Whales! Strange and Wonderful*. Honesdale, PA: Boyds Mills.

Raschka, Chris. 1998. *Arlene Sardine*. New York: Orchard.

———. 2003. *Talk to Me About the Alphabet*. New York: Holt.

Richards, Jean. 2003. *How the Elephant Got Its Trunk*. New York: Holt.

Roome, Diana Reynolds. 2003. *The Elephant's Pillow*. New York: Farrar, Straus, and Giroux.

Rose, Deborah Lee. 2003. *One Nighttime Sea*. New York: Scholastic.

Ross, Tony. 2002. *Centipede's 100 Shoes*. New York: Holt.

San Souci, Robert D. 2003. *Little Pierre: A Cajun Story from Louisiana*. San Diego: Harcourt.

Sandin, Joan. 2003. *Coyote School News*. New York: Henry Holt.

Schotter, Roni. 2003. *Captain Bob Takes Flight*. New York: Atheneum.

Schwartz, Amy. 2003. *What James Likes Best*. New York: Atheneum.

Shaw, Nancy. 2003. *Raccoon Tune*. New York: Holt.

Shepard, Aaron. 2003. *The Princess Mouse*. New York: Atheneum.

Shields, Carol Diggory. 2003. *Almost Late to School and More School Poems*. New York: Dutton.

Singer, Marilyn. 2003. *Fireflies at Midnight*. New York: Atheneum.

Smith, Charles R. 2003. *Hoop Queens*. Cambridge, MA: Candlewick.

Smith, William Jay. 2003. *Up the Hill and Down: Poems for the Very Young*. Honesdale, PA: Boyds Mills.

Sobel, June. 2003. *B Is for Bulldozer: A Construction ABC*. San Diego: Harcourt.

Sobol, Richard. 2003. *Adelina's Whales*. New York: Dutton.

Spinelli, Eileen. 2003. *The Perfect Thanksgiving*. New York: Holt.

———. 2003. *Rise the Moon*. New York: Dial.

Stadler, Alexander. 2003. *Beverly Billingsly Takes a Bow*. San Diego: Harcourt.

Stark, Ken. 2003. *Oh, Brother!* New York: Putnam.

Stephens, Helen. 2001. *Blue Horse*. New York: Scholastic.

Stevens, Janet, and Susan Stevens Crummel. 2003. *Jackalope*. San Diego: Harcourt.

Suen, Anastasia. 2003. *Raise the Roof!* New York: Viking.

Swift, Fran. 2003. *Old Blue Buggy*. New York: Dutton.

Swinburne, Stephen R. 2003. *Black Bear: North America's Bear*. Honesdale, PA: Boyds Mills.

Symes, Ruth. 2003. *The Sheep Fairy: When Wishes Have Dreams*. New York: Scholastic.

Tanaka, Shelley. 2002. *New Dinos*. New York: Atheneum.

Taulbert, Clifton. 2002. *Little Cliff and the Cold Place*. New York: Dial.

Taylor, Thomas. 2002. *The Loudest Roar*. New York: Scholastic.

Teague, Mark. 2002. *Dear Mrs. LaRue: Letters from Obedience School*. New York: Scholastic.

Thayer, Ernest L. 2003. *Casey at the Bat*. New York: Simon and Schuster.

Thompson, Pat. 2003. *Drat That Fat Cat*. New York: Scholastic.

U'Ren, Andrean 2003. *Mary Smith*. New York: Farrar, Straus, and Giroux.

Van Leeuwen, Jean. 2003. *The Amazing Air Balloon*. New York: Putnam.

Ward, Helen. 2003. *The Dragon Machine*. New York: Dutton.

Weston, Tamson. 2003. *Hey, Pancakes!* San Diego: Harcourt.

Wheeler, Lisa. 2003. *Avalanche Annie: A Not-So-Tall Tale*. San Diego: Harcourt.

———. 2003. *One Dark Night*. San Diego: Harcourt.

Widman, Christine. 2003. *Cornfield Hide-and-Seek*. New York: Farrar, Straus, and Giroux.

Wiles, Deborah. 2003. *One Wide Sky*. San Diego: Harcourt.

Wilson, Karma. 2003. *Bear Wants More*. New York: Simon and Schuster (McElderry).

Wolf, Allan. 2003. *The Blood-Hungry Spleen*. Cambridge, MA: Candlewick.

Wong, Janet S. 2003. *Minn and Jake*. New York: Farrar, Straus, and Giroux.

Wood, Audrey. 2003. *Alphabet Mystery*. New York: Scholastic.

Wood, Douglas. 2003. *Old Turtle and the Broken Truth*. New York: Scholastic.

Yee, Wong Herbert. 2003. *Tracks in the Snow*. New York: Henry Holt.

Yolen, Jane. 1998. *Raising Yoder's Barn*. New York: Little, Brown.

———. 2003. *Least Things: Poems About Small Natures*. Honesdale, PA: Boyds Mills.

———. 2003. *Roanoke: The Lost Colony*. New York: Simon and Schuster.

References

Alverman, D. 1984. "Teaching the Process of Inferring Through a Listening Guide." *Reading Horizons* 24 (4): 243–48.

Armstrong, W. 1997–1998. "Learning to Listen." *American Educator* 21: 24–25, 47.

Boodt, G. 1984. "Critical Listeners Become Critical Readers in Reading Class." *The Reading Teacher* 37 (4): 390–94.

Brown, S. L. 1991. *Improving Listening Skills in Young Children*. ERIC Document Reproduction Service No. ED 339 058.

Buttery, T. J., and P. J. Anderson. 1980. "Listen and Learn!" *Curriculum Review* 19 (4): 319–22.

Choate, J., and T. Rakes. 1987. "The Structured Listening Activity: A Model for Improving Listening Comprehension." *The Reading Teacher* 41: 194–99.

Colorado Model Content Standards for Reading and Writing. 1995. Denver: Colorado Department of Education.

Crum, G. 1989. "Listening Lesson Plans." *The Reading Teacher* 42 (4): 338–39.

Cunningham, P. 1975. "Transferring Comprehension from Listening to Reading." *The Reading Teacher* 29: 169–72.

Daneman, M. 1991. "Individual Differences in Reading Skills." In *Handbook of Reading Research*, Vol. 2, ed. R. Barr, M. Kamill, P. Mosenthal, and P. D. Pearson. White Plains, NY: Longman.

DeHaven, E. 1989. *Teaching and Learning the Language Arts*. 3d ed. New York: Scott, Foresman.

Devine, T. 1978. "Listening: What Do We Know After Fifty Years of Research and Theorizing?" *Journal of Reading* 21: 296–304.

———. 1982. *Listening Skills Schoolwide: Activities and Programs*. Urbana, IL: ERIC/National Council of Teachers of English.

Donahue, M. 1997. "Beliefs About Listening in Students with Learning Disabilities: Is the Speaker Always Right?" *Topics in Language Disorders* 17 (3): 41–61.

Duke, N. K., and P. D. Pearson. 2002. "Effective Practices for Developing Reading Comprehension." In *What Research Has to Say About Reading Instruction*, 3d ed., ed. A. E. Farstrup and S. J. Samuels, 205–42. Newark, DE: International Reading Association.

Elley, W. 1989. "Vocabulary Acquisition from Listening to Stories." *Reading Research Quarterly* 24: 174–87.

Faber, A., and E. Mazlish. 1987. "How to Talk So Students Will Listen and Listen So Students Will Talk." *American Educator* 11: 37–42.

Foulke, E. 1968. "Listening Comprehension as a Function of Word Rate." *Journal of Communication* 18: 198–206.

Funk, H., and G. Funk. 1989. "Guidelines for Developing Listening Skills." *The Reading Teacher* 42: 660–63.

Galvin, K. 1985. *Listening by Doing: Developing Effective Listening Skills.* Lincolnwood, IL: National Textbook.

Garman, C. G., and J. F. Carman. 1992. *Teaching Young Children Effective Listening Skills.* York, PA: William Gladden Foundation.

Goss, B. 1982. "Listening as Information Processing." *Communication Quarterly* 30 (4): 304–307.

Goulden, N. 1998. "The Roles of National and State Standards in Implementing Speaking, Listening, and Media Literacy." *Communication Education* 47: 194–208.

Harnishfeger, L. 1980. *Listening Activities for Young Children.* Denver, CO: Love.

Harris, T., and R. Hodges. 1995. *The Literacy Dictionary: The Vocabulary of Reading and Writing.* Newark, DE: International Reading Association.

Hunsaker, R. A. 1990. *Understanding and Developing Skills of Oral Communication.* Englewood, CO: Morton.

Imhof, M. 2000. *How to Monitor Listening More Efficiently: Metacognitive Sttrategies.* ERIC Document Reproduction Service No. 438 583.

Jalongo, M. R. 1995. "Promoting Active Listening in the Classroom." *Childhood Education* 72 (1): 13–18.

———. 1996. "Teaching Young Children to Become Better Listeners." *Young Children* 51 (2): 21–26.

———. 2003. *Early Childhood Language Arts.* 3d ed. New York: Allyn and Bacon.

Janeczko, P. 2003. *Opening a Door: Reading Poetry in the Middle School Classroom.* New York: Scholastic.

Levesque, J. 1989. "ELVES: A Read–Aloud Strategy to Develop Listening Comprehension." *The Reading Teacher* 43: 93–94.

Lundsteen, S. 1979. *Listening: Its Impact on Reading and the Other Language Art.* Urbana, IL: National Council of Teachers of English.

———. 1990. "Learning to Listen and Learning to Read." In *Perspectives of Talk and Learning*, ed. S. Hynds and D. L. Rubin. Urbana, IL: National Council of Teachers of English.

McDevitt, T. 1990. "Encouraging Young Children's Listening." *Academic Therapy* 25 (5): 569–77.

McSportan, E. 1997. "Towards Better Listening and Learning in the Classroom." *Educational Review* 49 (1): 13–21.

Moffett, J., and B. J. Wagner. 1992. *Student-Centered Language Arts, K–12*. Portsmouth, NH: Heinemann.

National Communication Association. 1996. Washington, DC: National Communication Association.

Neilsen, L. 1991. "Is Anyone Listening?" *The Reading Teacher* 44: 494–96.

Opitz, M. 1989. An Investigation of the Importance of Using Student Interviews in the Development of Chapter I Diagnostic Profiles. Ph.D. diss., University of Oregon, Eugene.

———. 2000. *Rhymes and Reasons: Literature and Language Play for Phonological Awareness*. Portsmouth, NH: Heinemann.

Paley, V. G. 1986. "On Listening to What Children Say." *Harvard Educational Review* 56 (2): 122–31.

Pearson, P. David, and L. Fielding. 1982. "Research Update: Listening Comprehension." *Language Arts* 59: 617–29.

Pinnell, G., and A. Jaggar. 2003. "Oral Language: Speaking and Listening in Elementary Classrooms." In *Handbook of Research on Teaching the English Language Arts*, 2 ed., ed. J. Flood, D. Lapp, J. Squire, and J. Jensen, 881–914. Mahwah, NJ: Lawrence Erlbaum.

Rost, M. 1990. *Listening in Language Learning*. New York: Longman.

———. 1991. *Listening in Action: Activities for Developing Listening in Language Teaching*. New York: Prentice Hall.

Rubin, D. 2000. *Teaching Elementary Language Arts*. 6th ed. New York: Allyn and Bacon.

Samuels, S. J. 1984. "Factors Influencing Listening: Inside and Outside the Head." *Theory into Practice* 23 (3): 183–89.

Strother, D. B. 1987. "Practical Applications of Research on Listening." *Phi Delta Kappan* 68: 625–28.

Swafford, J., and T. Paulos. 1993. "Creating Experiences for Listening and Learning." *Reading Horizons* 33 (5): 401–17.

Swanson, C. 1997. *Who's Listening in the Classroom: A Research Paradigm*. ERIC Document Reproduction Service No. 407 659.

Tompkins, G. 2002. *Language Arts: Content and Teaching Strategies*. 5th ed. New York: Merrill/Prentice Hall.

Winn, D. 1988. "Develop Listening Skills as a Part of the Curriculum." *The Reading Teacher* 42 (2): 144–46.

Wolvin, A., and C. Coakley. 1979. *Listening Instruction*. Urbana, IL: National Council of Teachers of English.

———. 1996. *Listening*. 5th ed. Madison, WI: Brown and Benchmark.

Wright, J., and L. Laminak. 1982. "First Graders Can Be Critical Listeners and Readers." *Language Arts* 59: 133–36.

Zbaracki, M. 2003. A Descriptive Study of How Humorous Children's Literature Serves to Engage Children in Reading. Ph.D. diss., The Ohio State University, Columbus.